HOW THE PARTHENON WAS BUILT

HOW THE PARTHENON WAS BUILT

STUDIES IN THE RELATIONSHIP BETWEEN THE PARTHENON AND ITS PREDECESSOR

by J.B.LYNN

SWAN PUBLISHING

First published 2006
Swan Publishing
PO Box 120,
Berwick-upon-Tweed, TD15 9AE.

Printed by
Martins the Printers Ltd., Berwick-upon-Tweed, TD15 1RS.

Typeset by Simprim Studios

A catalogue record for this book is available from the British Library.

ISBN   0-9550864-1-8   Cloth
ISBN   0-9550864-2-6   P.bk

FOR MARI

CONTENTS

CONTENTS

ILLUSTRATED GLOSSARY OF TEMPLE COMPONENTS

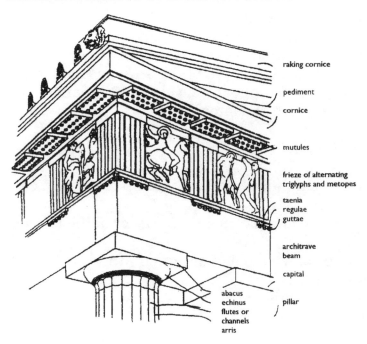

raking cornice

pediment

cornice

mutules

frieze of alternating
triglyphs and metopes

taenia
regulae
guttae

architrave
beam

capital

abacus
echinus
flutes or
channels
arris

pillar

PLAN OF EARLIER PARTHENON

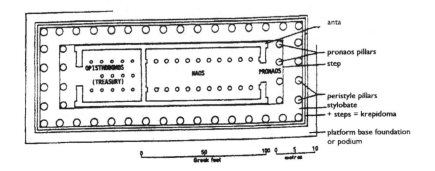

OPISTHODOMOS
(TREASURY)

NAOS

PRONAOS

anta

pronaos pillars

step

peristyle pillars
stylobate
+ steps = krepidoma

platform base foundation
or podium

0   50   100   0   5   10
         Greek foot   metres

ACKNOWLEDGEMENTS

This text has gone through several versions since it began as a lecture in 1986. At every stage there has been valuable help, advice and encouragement from family, friends and acquaintances. On reading an early draft Prof. Guy Oddie usefully reminded me of the advice of Quiller-Couch to 'murder your darlings'. Prof. Richard Tomlinson kindly signalled another version as worth developing. My friend Selwyn Goldsmith read a number of early drafts and when a title was being considered the one adopted was suggested by him. Prof. Andrew Ballantyne attended the original lecture and has maintained his interest in the developing text. I have benefited over many years from the University of Newcastle library's Ancient History and Archaeology collection assembled largely by Prof. Brian Shefton, initially encouraged by Vice-Chancellor Charles Bosanquet whose father had been Director of the British School at Athens, 1900-5. References not obtainable there were supplied by my daughter Inez from the London Library and by John Perkins of the Warburg Institute. I am indebted to old colleagues Edward Bird and Bruce Thompson, at the time structural engineers with the Ryder Company, for their analysis of the stresses and strains within the crane design and their advice on how to resolve them. In addition to taking the photographs and copying the figures drawn by the author, Fiona Manzeh-Longbone has managed the metamorphosis of the text into its present format and I am grateful for that as I am to Inez for all her help and encouragement with earlier versions of the book and to my son Jonathan for supplying a copy of Penrose. I am grateful for the permission of the German Archaeological Institute in Athens to use their archive photographs for figure 6 and to the Bibliothèque National de France for permission to reproduce the Carrey drawings in their possession. Professor Lothar Haselberger has permitted me to reproduce as figure 8 his drawing of Didyma which opened up a new avenue of exploration of how Athenian architects conveyed their requirements to the workmen on the site. Anyone writing about the Parthenon is obliged to acknowledge the work produced by the teams of scholars, craftsmen and others engaged in the conservation work proceeding on the Athenian Akropolis. I gladly join them and look forward to a full exposition of what those teams have discovered and recorded in their practical studies. The translation of Plutarch is by Ian Scott-Kilvert 'The Rise and Fall of Athens' Penguin Books 1960. The translation from the French of Le Corbusier's 'Towards a New Architecture' is by Frederick Etchells The Architectural Press 1970.

FIGURES

FIGURES (cont'd)

STUDY 3   PRECISION, SUBTLETY AND ABERRATION
                IN THE DESIGN OF THE PARTHENON

.

FIGURES (cont'd)

STUDY 4   THE DESIGN OF THE EARLIER PARTHENON

FIGURES (cont'd)

STUDY 5   THE ARCHITECTS

PLATES

PLATE I. SCULPTURED FIGURES FROM THE PEDIMENTS OF TEMPLES DESTROYED BY THE PERSIANS IN 480 BC
DISCOVERED ON THE AKROPOLIS DURING EXCAVATION OF 1885-90

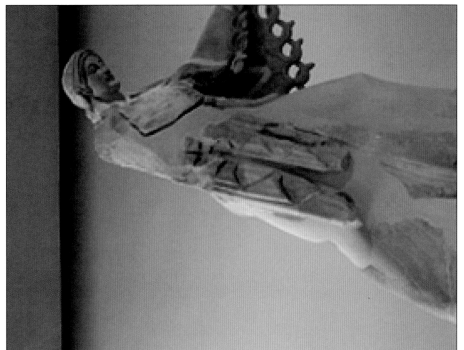

PLATE 2 PROFILES OF DORIC CAPITALS COMPARED

Taken from a pillar on Temple of Aphaia on Aigina and now resting on the stylobate

Taken from pillars of the Parthenon, awaiting restoration

PLATE 3 UPWARD CURVE ON STYLOBATE AND STEPS ON
EAST FRONT OF PARTHENON

PLATE 4 EAST END OF AKROPOLIS SHOWING THE CAVE BEYOND THE AGLAURION

In 480 BC the boundary wall was much lower than at present allowing Persian entry after a difficult climb

PLATE 5 BOTH EARLIER AND PRESENT PARTHENONS WERE FOUNDED ON A HIGH PLINTH BUILT IN THE 480'S BC TO BRING THE TEMPLE INTO PROMINENCE FOR THE CITIZENS BELOW

Temple of Aphaia, Aigina

The Propylaia

The Erechtheion

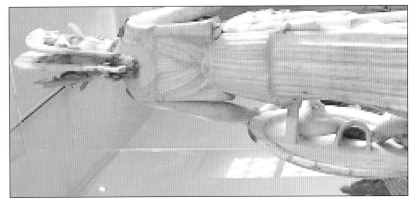

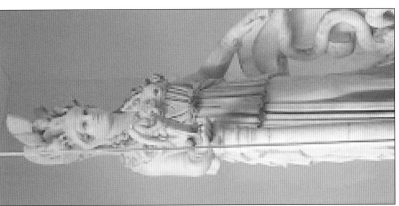

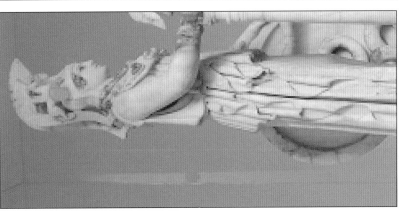

PLATE 7 MODEL OF THE ATHENE FIGURE FOR THE PARTHENON COMPLETED IN 438 BC.

PLATE 8 ASPASIA AND FRIENDS?

PLATE 9 LIFTING AND PLACING ALREADY FLUTED DRUMS OF STONE

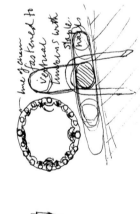

Method in use in early December 2004

Speculative note of how it could have been done

May 1998

In order to move the fluted stones of the Areos Hera had to be a method of lifting them vertically the temple structure to disengage the dowel pins and to lower them again in the new location.

The relative weight of these drums to those on the P would be

D = 1.1m   height say .9m.   P = 1.9   x .9m.   Parthenon

$\pi r^2 H$

= 1.555 m³

= 4,276 Kcg.

= 4.276 tonnes

(say 2,750 kg/per m³)

7.686 m³.

+ mantle say .025 x .9 x 5.97   2πr

= .134 m³

2.820 m³

= 7,755 Kg.

= 7.755 tonnes

A sling of chains surrounding a ring of flat timbers were placed around the drum and tapered wedges inserted vertically between the timbers and the stone and driven down to tighten the chain around the ring of timbers

had groove fastened to vertical timbers with straps (nails)

PLATE 10 WEST FACE OF EREKHTHEION

PLATE 11 BASE OF IONIC PILLARS ON EREKHTHEION NORTH PORCH

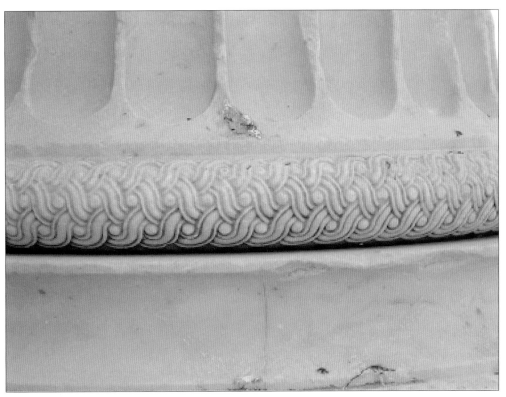

PLATE 12   SOUTH FLANK OF EREKHTHEION

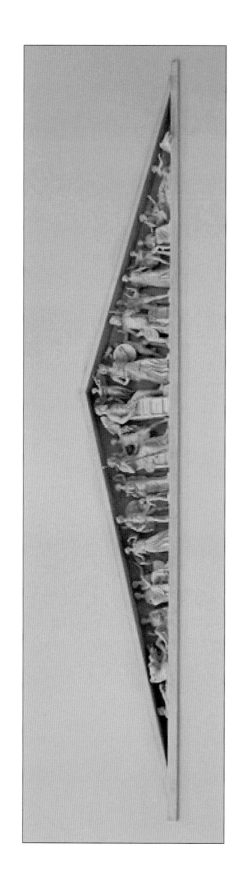

PLATE 13 MODELS OF PEDIMENT SCULPTURES (RECONSTRUCTED) ON THE PARTHENON EXHIBITED IN THE AKROPOLIS MUSEUM

PLATE 14 THE LATER PARTHENON WAS ERECTED AS FAR WEST AS POSSIBLE ON THE OLD FOUNDATION

PLATE 15 PART OF FLANK FRIEZE OF THE PARTHENON IN THE BRITISH MUSEUM

PLATE 16 PART OF EAST FRIEZE OF THE PARTHENON IN THE BRITISH MUSEUM

Hera

Zeus

PREFACE

In his brief biography of Perikles, the Greek historian Plutarch, who had studied in Athens around AD 66, described the visual impact of the buildings which the Athenian leader had erected on the Akropolis in the 5th. century BC. in these terms;

"Each one possessed a beauty which seemed venerable the moment it was born, and at the same time a youthful vigour which makes them appear to this day as if they were newly built. A bloom of eternal freshness hovers over these works of his and preserves them from the touch of time, as if some unfading spirit of youth, some ageless vitality had been breathed into them."

As well as his own experience of the buildings as he remembered them from his student days, Plutarch was reflecting accounts of the temples which were still available to him but which no longer survive for us, impressions written when the buildings were still new.

Le Corbusier, a Swiss architect, also wrote about the Parthenon as part of what he intended to be the gospel of modern architecture, 'Vers une Architecture' 1923;

"There has been nothing like it anywhere or at any period. It happened at a moment when things were at their keenest, when a

1

man, stirred by the noblest thoughts, crystallized them in a plastic work of light and shade. The mouldings of the Parthenon are infallible and implacable. In severity they go far beyond our practice, or man's normal capabilities. Here, the purest witness to the physiology of sensation, and to the mathematical speculation attached to it, is fixed and determined: we are riveted by our senses; we are ravished in our minds; we touch the axis of harmony. No question of religious dogma enters in; no symbolic description, no naturalistic representation; there is nothing but pure forms in precise relationships."

As a student of architecture in 1944, I read these words and wondered; how can the Parthenon evoke such reverential response from an ancient Greek, praising a building which was already five hundred years old, and also from a twentieth century Swiss architect enthusing about the severely blast-damaged remains of the temple? How is it possible for an architect to imbue inert stone with such a moving spirit of freshness and youthful vitality? For a keen student of architecture, that was the essential goal to be pursued in one's studies. How were these qualities, perceived in the nave of Durham Cathedral, in the setting and complex form of Bamburgh Castle, in the spatial arrangement, inside and out, of Vanbrugh's Seaton Delaval Hall, to be built into one's own designs?

It was not possible at the time to see for myself whether Plutarch's and Le Corbusier's eulogies were well founded, but a visit to the Athenian Akropolis some years later convinced me that the two authors were not exaggerating. What I experienced there also persuaded me that both writers were correct in assigning to the sculptor Pheidias the principal role in the creation of this great temple. Here was a building which was much more than the product of applying the rules of a supposed Greek canon of design. The Temple of Hephaistos, overlooking the Athenian Agora, may be cited as a canonical work, but not the Parthenon. What was it that made the difference? And how could Pheidias, a busy sculptor, have had such an influence upon the building of a huge temple? This was not his sphere of work; he was a cutter of stone, a modeller in clay and a highly skilled foundryman. What were the circumstances and the personal relationships at the time which could allow this to happen? As a young man I felt instinctively that the style of writing about ancient architecture in terms of the evolution of forms, as if they conformed to Darwin's view of natural species, failed to recognize what really happened when new forms were being made. These were the works of men, men of passion, men with 'nous', open to new ways of thinking, having new visions, without in any way devaluing the traditions and work of their fathers. So what was the story that lay behind the influence Pheidias had on the design of these marvellous works of architecture? How had it come about? As a perpetual student of the art, and a practising architect over the next fifty years, these were questions which persisted, questions which could only be answered, so far as they related to the Parthenon, by closer study. The aim of this book is to present those of my studies which provide answers to some of these questions, and suggest answers to others, although these turned out to be not always what I would have expected.

Some of the visitors to the Parthenon in the early 19th century thought they had found the answer to the first of them, 'what made the Parthenon so special?' C.R. Cockerell, destined to be professor of architecture at the Royal Academy, 1840-57, spent the years 1810-17 on an extended tour of ancient sites in Greece, Asia Minor, Sicily and Italy becoming, with his colleague Allason, the first to detect entasis, a slight swelling on the outline of the pillars. The English architect John Pennethorne, knowing of Cockerell's findings, was the first to discover the rising curvature of the stylobate in 1832, but was beaten to the publishers by Joseph Hoffer, who was then the newly appointed German architect in charge of Athenian classical remains. It was thought that these refinements, including the inward inclination of the pillars, must be the explanation of the powerful appeal which the temple exercised upon all who saw it. Cockerell realised that a more detailed study was necessary. The area around the temple had, by the mid-1840's, been cleared of the encumbrance of Turkish structures which earlier had prevented any precise survey of the remains of the fabric being made. Cockerell persuaded Francis Penrose to carry out the task. He was a young architect who became a scholar interested in ancient architecture, and in 1842 was appointed travelling bachelor of the University of Cambridge, visiting Athens for the first time in 1845. After careful preparation, he recorded his measurements during a second visit in 1846-7, when he was accompanied by his friend Thomas Willson. His primary interest lay in these refinements which the designers of the 5th century BC. had given their structures. They are all of such subtlety that Penrose was obliged to design and carry out his survey with a degree of thoroughness and precision capable of revealing them. He recorded profiles only where they were perfectly preserved; he noted accurately all misalignments caused by earthquake or explosive shock, so that from his measured drawings it is possible to separate wrought form from accidental effect.

He recorded his measurements in an unusual numerical language. Nearly a hundred years earlier two British architects, James Stuart and Nicholas Revett, had visited Athens and made measurements of Greek temple remains, publishing their findings, including dimensioned drawings, with the help of the Dilettante Society in 1762. Although those two men were unaware of the refinements which had drawn them to the Greek temples, they had realised that the English units of feet and fractions of inches were too unwieldy a way of recording any extended series of measurements. Taking a lead from their practice, Penrose used a system of feet and a thousand parts of a foot, and had measuring rods specially made for the purpose, which delivered a precision similar to dividing an eighth of an inch by about ten, or a millimetre by something over three. It was never a system of measurement in common currency, and this may explain why, while Penrose's text was widely studied at the time of its publication in 1851, his detailed dimensional observations on Athenian architecture of the 5th century BC., illustrated in the plates which followed, have not been thoroughly studied until the advent of the calculating machine; this allowed an easy translation into metric measure to be made which offered a ready access to his work denied to earlier generations of scholars.[1]

As the Parthenon stones have been disturbed twice since Penrose measured them, his precise record is of supreme importance in any attempt to understand the building. The studies which follow rely on his drawn and dimensioned account of the structure. When Balanos, the superintendent of works on the Akropolis, carried out his partial restoration of the remains of the temple in the 1920's, which involved renewing the iron cramps connecting the stones one to another, he made his own drawings, recording his measurements in metric dimensions.[2] These do not always accord with the metric translations of those made by Penrose, which were of greater precision. Manolis Korres, the architect responsible for the restoration work carried out on the temple in the 1980's and 90's, which entails among other conservation measures replacing the rusting cramps

---

[1] Penrose's work is not included in the lengthy bibliography of 'The Athenian Akropolis' by Jeffrey M. Hurwit. University of Oregon 1999.
[2] N.Balanos 'Les Monuments de l'Acropole' Paris 1938.

which Balanos had used with new ones of titanium, recognises the true value of Penrose's survey and has acknowledged its worth.[3]   Any student of the architecture of the Parthenon, as found in the 1840's, is obliged to turn to what is still the only major, coherent and comprehensive source of knowledge about it;   'An Investigation of the Principles of Athenian Architecture' by Francis Cranmer Penrose,   published by the Society of Dilettanti in 1851.

But there was much more information to be quarried from Penrose's accurate recording of what remained of the Parthenon in 1846-7.   As well as establishing the degree of refinement of line, form and colour embodied in the Parthenon, his survey also pointed, by implication, to how the building had been erected. The plates in the first edition illustrate clearly how the stylobate stones and the steps immediately below, together making up the krepidoma, were set to an arched curvature that was greater than that of the earlier profile of the podium platform which supported it.   They show how certain stones, those at the base of each pillar and those just below the capitals had their contact surfaces shaped to slopes in order to bring about the equal inclination of the pillars.   Hitherto these drawings have never been used to explain the construction process and sequence; possibly because only a practising architect would be curious enough to want to know, and have the necessary experience to recognise from the subtleties revealed in the dimensions on the drawings how the stones must have been worked and placed in position.

As well as leaving clues to how the temple could have been built, the detailed evidence of Penrose's survey also revealed that there

---

[3] Manolis M. Korres 'Acropolis Restoration - Recent Discoveries on the Acropolis'1995 p.1

were many strange aberrations of detail in the less visible parts of an otherwise perfect temple which, hitherto, have remained unremarked and unexplained, even by Penrose himself. Just as a radiograph of a painting can reveal how it has been worked or reworked, the detailed studies which follow explore these anomalies and, in the process, propose the most likely reason for them. In so doing they uncover a surprising aspect of the history of the building which some scholars, notably Rhys Carpenter[4] and J.A. Bundgaard,[5] have in the past suspected but were unable to substantiate with acceptable evidence. This is that the temple was in fact built twice. The first version was started in 488 BC to celebrate the victory at Marathon. In 480 BC the little of it that existed was destroyed by the returning Persians; it appears that it was restarted around 467 BC and was largely completed by 448 BC. This temple is referred to in this book as the earlier Parthenon. Amazingly and, no doubt some would have said, perversely, it was then taken down stone by stone and re-erected, re-using most of the material, in enlarged and re-dimensioned form in order to accommodate the huge statue of Athene which the Athenians commissioned Pheidias to make for the temple. So the Parthenon as we know it is a rare example of a building which has been reworked with the intention of enhancing its impact.

There have been obstacles in the way of this perception. One was a lack of curiosity about the design of the earlier Parthenon following a study published by B.H. Hill in 1912,[6] a study which seems to have been accepted by almost all scholars of the subject as definitive, despite the fact that it ignored important archaeological evidence which it had reported, evidence which is

---

[4] 'The Architects of the Parthenon' 1970.
[5] 'Parthenon and the Mycenean City on the Heights' 1976
[6] 'The Older Parthenon' A.J.A. (American Journal of Archaeology) vol.XVI

crucial in establishing what the design of this earlier Parthenon could have been like. Another was the swaying back and forth of opinion concerning an oath allegedly taken before the battle at Plataia in 479 BC. Some scholars were persuaded to accept the view that the reported oath was genuine and included a clause vowing not to rebuild the temples destroyed by the Persians, and therefore there could not have been any temple building activity in Athens between 479 and 449 BC.[7] The evidence furnished here suggests that major temple building did in fact take place in Athens during those years, so altering the balance of the debate about the standing and the significance of the oath. It should also raise the more interesting question of how the myth of the oath could have arisen. Likewise our understanding of the background to and the nature of the political rivalry between Perikles and Thoukudides, son of Melesias, during the 440's and 430's BC would now be coloured by the discovery that a major temple, erected and presumably paid for by the conservative families within Athenian society, to which Thoukudides belonged, was in 447 BC taken down and replaced at considerable public expense for, what must have seemed to his rivals, no better reason than to glorify Perikles and strengthen his political ascendancy.

A third has been a tendency to attribute to the 5th century Greek temple architects certain Vitruvian principles of design. These architects were practising nearly five hundred years before Vitruvius. There could be no Roman influence in 5th century Athens, and it is a mistake to suppose that Vitruvius, despite relying heavily on Greek precedent in many branches of engineering and later Hellenistic architecture, could have derived his rules of design directly from 5th century Athenian practice. So it is important that we try not to look at Athenian buildings of

---

[7] Summarised by R. Meiggs in Appendix 10A of 'The Athenian Empire' 1972

that era through Roman eyes. Nor should we bring to them attitudes which were completely alien to the Athenian culture, when pragmatism and flair would have debarred the formulating and application of strict rules concerning architecture, despite their acceptance of tradition, which remained a powerful force. (That is why the spelling of proper names adopted in the text which follows has sought, not always successfully, to be free from the contamination of later Latinised versions.[8] It is simply a token of the chronology.)

The studies for this book have entailed translating Penrose's decimalised version of the English foot measure into the European metric system of dimensioning, in order to make them more widely understood. Where aggregates of Penrose's dimensions were involved, the adding and subtracting has been carried out, wherever practicable, in the foot measure and only the final total translated into metric; this procedure reduces the minor but cumulative errors of aggregating many individually translated components.

---

[8] For instance, the spelling of the historian Thucydides's name has been kept in the form which is more familiar to his English readers, to distinguish him from his namesake, Thoukudides, son of Melesias.

INTRODUCTION

The building of the temple we now know as the Parthenon was started in 447 BC. There is a sense in which the history of the building goes back to 547 BC.,[9] for it was then that the reason for its erection began to take shape. It was in the middle of the 6th century BC that Cyrus, newly king not only of the Persians but of the Medes as well, having defeated the Median dynasty and taken over their empire, moved against his only serious rivals in the west, the notoriously wealthy Lydians centred on Sardis, and conquered them, thereby creating an empire two thousand miles in extent. The country of Lydia included Greek settlements along the Aegean seaboard of what is now south-west Turkey, whose people showed early resentment to the new rulers by joining an unsuccessful army of rebellion raised by a Lydian who had stolen back the Lydian gold. When the Greek settlers appealed for help from Sparta, the most powerful city in Greece at that time, there was no response.

Cyrus next subdued Babylon but ruled it as a benign deliverer, an efficacious technique he had developed from experience in the west. He died in 529 BC and was succeeded by his son Cambyses, who devoted much of his remaining life to the conquest of Egypt. When he died there was some confusion over who should succeed him, but a military coup led by Darius settled the matter. Darius married two of Cyrus's daughters to secure the royal succession and proceeded to stiffen the organisation of the Persian empire, a process which eventually again stirred up the rebellious Greeks of the Ionian and Carian

---

[9] There is another sense in which its history goes back to 566 BC., if the earlier Parthenon is simply seen as a replacement of an even earlier temple, the Hekatompedon, believed by Dinsmoor and others to have been built on the same site to celebrate the inauguration of the Panathenaic festival on that date.

shores.   This time their appeal for aid brought Athenians and men from Eretria in ships who helped them to capture and destroy Sardis, which had been the capital of Lydia but was then a Persian city.

Darius, who had been enlarging his empire eastward into the Punjab and northward into Europe, sought revenge.   His forces sailed westward to mainland Greece, punishing first Eretria, but his army was beaten by a smaller force of Athenians at the bay of Marathon in 490 BC.   Four years later, when Darius died, his eldest son Xerxes inherited the throne and the empire and he determined to avenge the humiliation inflicted on the Persians by the men of Athens.   According to Herodotos he amassed a huge army which increased in size as it moved west from Susa to the Mediterranean coast and then north to the Hellespont, which was crossed by a bridge of ships held together with cables of flax and papyrus   A formidable navy was assembled also, not only to supply the army but to challenge the Athenians at sea.

After Marathon, Themistokles, that most persuasive of Athenian leaders, had advised his compatriots to invest the proceeds of a strike of silver in a navy and, fortunately for them, they had heeded him.   The resulting fleet of 200 of the latest type of oared warships was the largest component in the navy assembled by the defensive alliance.   As the Persian-inspired horde advanced, checked only temporarily by a small force of Spartans at Thermopylai and a Greek navy at Artemision, helped by north wind storms, the Athenians evacuated their countryside of Attika sending the women and children to Troezen while the men retreated to the offshore island of Salamis, most of them manning the ships in the narrow straits between the island and the mainland.   There Xerxes's vast navy, watched by its king from the heights above the shore, was comprehensively routed. His army however went on to burn Athens and destroy all its temples, including the new temple intended to celebrate Marathon, a structure still in the earliest stage of erection. Xerxes himself fled back to Persia, but most of his army stayed on and was again, surprisingly, defeated by a combined Greek army under Spartan leadership at the battle outside Plataia. Meanwhile a Greek fleet had sailed to Delos and thence to the island of Samos opposite the Ionian mainland. From there they won a battle against the Persians at Mykale, about the same time as the victory on land at Plataia. The Athenians harassed the retreating Persians out of Greece, out of the islands of the Aegean sea and, as the years passed, harried them from the old Greek coastal settlements of Asia Minor as far as Cyprus, even pursuing them across the sea to Egypt. Kimon, son of the Marathon victor, Miltiades, led many of these annual campaigns, which were very profitable.

Sparta did not show any strong interest in following up the success they had shared in at Mykale, and it was left to the Athenians to assume leadership of the liberated cities of the Aegean, some in Thrace and others along the Propontis as far as Byzantion. An alliance was quickly formed, a negotiated process in which the Athenian general Aristeides played a prominent part. The league was dominated by Athenians but took its name from the sacred island of Delos where the common treasury was established.

Xerxes was assassinated in 465 BC. His second son Artaxerxes had his elder brother and the assassin slain and became king himself at the age of eighteen. Shortly afterwards he received at his court Themistokles, who had been ostracised by the Athenians in 470 BC and later forced to flee Hellas altogether. Artaxerxes ruled Persia for the next forty-two years, eventually coming to terms with Athens, possibly around 448BC.

STUDY 1   **THE FOUNDATION**

The famous victory at Marathon, won by Athenians with help only from the men of Plataia, against the much larger Persian army commanded by Datis, was an astonishing deliverance from a terrible fate.[1] Earlier, despite six days of fierce resistance, the city of Eretria had been destroyed and its citizens enslaved by the Persians. After the battle, according to Plutarch's account,[2] substantial booty from the captured tents and ships was brought back to Athens by Aristeides, the general of the tribe Antiochis who, with his men, had been given the honourable if unenviable task of burying the dead.   The retrieval of the spoils of war may have played some part in his subsequent election as 'archon eponymos' in 489/8 BC. During his year of office he probably promoted the idea of celebrating the victory by erecting a new, large temple to the city's patron goddess Athene.

If, as Dinsmoor has suggested,[3] the temple foundation was set out in the late summer of 488 BC., then the next five or six years were spent in building a large foundation platform, a structure of solid masonry to support the temple on a rocky site which sloped away towards the west and, more steeply, to the south. This foundation required substantially more stone for its construction

---

[1] J.F. Lazenby 'The Defence of Greece' p.46-7.

[2] 'Aristeides' 5.

[3] see W.B.Dinsmoor 'The Date of the Older Parthenon' A.J.A. 1934 p.447. (Both Hill and Dinsmoor referred to the earlier Parthenon as the Older Parthenon.) This paper summarised the conflicting interpretations of the architectural evidence, and surveyed the evidence of the potsherds found among the fill material used to the south of the temple foundation in the light of Graef and Langlotz's study of these Athenian vase fragments (1909-1933) to substantiate his conclusions that the foundation was dated between 490 and 480 BC. He used astronomical evidence   based on the orientation of the temple, which had been measured by Penrose, to determine that the axis and the perimeter of the foundation were staked out at sunrise on August 31st. 488 BC., the time and date of the Panathenaic procession.

than did the temple which was to stand upon it, with the result that when the Persians returned in 480 BC little of the new temple had been erected, only the krepidoma, the three steps forming a base, and on it the lower marble drums of some of the pillars. Timber scaffolding and lifting gear for manoeuvring these stones into place must have been in position; this is known from the number of fire damaged stones which resulted from its firing. Most of the parts of that temple which had been standing above the steps, together with the completed shrines and votive figures dating from the sixth century, were physically destroyed or scarred by the conflagration.

It was established many years ago that a rebuilding of the temple now known as the Parthenon was commenced in 447 BC, as part of an ambitious public works programme initiated by Perikles and, since he had promoted it, he was made responsible to the Athenian assembly for its general management. Work on that building was completed in 438 BC, exactly fifty years after the foundation for the temple had been first set out, and a huge figure of Athene the virgin goddess, a timber framed structure faced with ivory and gold, was dedicated within it. The sculptural enrichments of the gable pediments at each end of the temple then began. At the same time a new and enlarged gateway at the entrance to the Akropolis, known as the Propylaia, was started. This building was never completed and further work on it was abandoned in 432 BC when war with Sparta was imminent.

The subsequent story of the temple which we know as the Parthenon is well documented elsewhere:[4] beginning as a celebration of victory over the Persians built in honour of the city's patron goddess, it became in turn a Christian church for a

[4] Jeffrey M. Hurwit 'The Athenian Acropolis' C.U.P. 1999.

thousand years, then a mosque, next and fatally a Turkish magazine, destroyed eventually by a spectacular explosion in 1687, caused by a Venetian bombardment during their war with the Ottoman Empire.   Later it was used as a quarry and is now probably the most famous ruin ever made, visited by people young and old from every continent.

It is its rediscovery which concerns us here, because that process brought to light the evidence of the earlier version of the temple and first raised the question, never answered satisfactorily because it was never adequately framed, 'what was the relationship between the two projects?'

(1)   The process of discovery

In defining what Athenian buildings might have looked like in the 5th century BC., the British architects Stuart and Revett played a notable part in the 18th century, followed by Cockerell in the early 19th, but the liberation of Greece in 1832 meant that the Greeks themselves now wished to discover their own inheritance, and by 1837 they had established the Greek Archeological Society. It was this urge which began the process of uncovering, back through time, the layers of historical accretion which hid what they were looking for.   They were reaching back to the days when Athens had been most glorious, an age which inspired not only Greeks but civilised men and women of every nation who could help in the research.

One of the earliest on the scene was an English soldier, W.M.Leake, who in 1799 had been instructing Turkish troops at Constantinople before turning classical topographer in Greece. He resided there 1808-10 and published his 'Topography of Athens' in 1821.   At the time the only physical evidence of ancient Greek building and the temple destruction within the Akropolis consisted of sparse remains of the Erekhtheion, fragments of the Propylaia, heavily encumbered with Turkish walls, the ruined Parthenon and two sets of architectural features built into the north perimeter wall of the former sanctuary. Those nearer the east end included marble blocks and marble drums with a diameter of about 2 metres, intended as base stones for Doric pillars, which had the typical flutes or scalloped profiles cut into one end to a height of a few centimetres. Many of these stones exhibited signs of fire damage. Near the west end of the wall, facing over the city, were sections of Doric entablatures consisting of cornice stones, alternating triglyphs and metopes from the frieze courses and lengths of architrave beams below, mostly made of stone from Peirieus, and all having suffered structural damage. Leake surmised that the marble drums and the stone entablatures had belonged to an earlier temple built somewhere on the Akropolis and destroyed by the Persians in 480 BC. There was no sign then of the foundation of the Parthenon, and the Turkish structures over much of the Akropolis were preventing its discovery.

On winning their independence the Greeks selected a Bavarian prince as king, and this brought other Germans to administrative posts in the government of the country. Joseph Hoffer became architect in charge of Athenian classical remains in 1833 and within a very short time a fellow countryman, Professor Ludwig Ross was given permission to excavate south of the Parthenon, in collaboration with the Greek archaeologist Kyriakos Pittakis. They noted that the general ground level around the temple was at the level of the second marble step below the perimeter pillars. After discovering that a stone foundation extended some 2 metres beyond the lowest of three

Fig. I SKETCH BY PENROSE OF THE NORTH WALL OF THE AKROPOLIS

Fig. 2 MEASURED DRAWINGS BY PENROSE OF ENTABLATURES BUILT INTO THE NORTH WALL

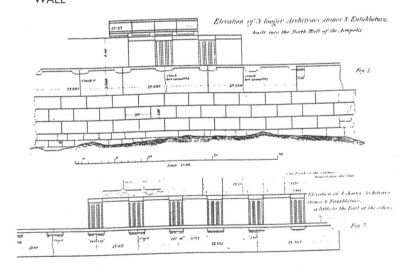

steps, Ross sank two pits, one near the south-west angle of the temple, reaching base rock at a depth of 5.5 metres and, in the process, discovered that there was a deep and continuous foundation platform supporting the Parthenon. The other, located at the south-east corner of this foundation, was at the time taken down to only 3 - 3.6 metres where an earth stratum was uncovered which was mixed with charcoal, broken archaic bronze figurines, fragments of painted roof tiles and other debris. He deduced that this had been cleared away from the buildings destroyed on the Akropolis by the Persians when they sacked Athens in 480 BC. The true depth of the foundation platform here was not investigated. Ross and Pittakis concluded that the temple destroyed by the Persians had been a complete and ancient one standing on the foundation which now supported the Parthenon, one which had been constructed with marble steps and pillars supporting an entablature mostly cut from the same kind of stone as those surviving pieces built into the north wall of the Akropolis after the Persians had been defeated. And, as there was no further evidence to show otherwise, for the next fifty years most scholars of the subject agreed.

In 1875 German archaeologists were given permission to excavate at Olympia and they proposed a new approach: to excavate the whole area systematically over a period of five years, noting everything they found from whatever era. Learning from this a similar large-scale investigation was started on the Athenian Akropolis in 1885, conducted by Kavvadias and recorded by Kawerau with sketches, notes, drawings and photographs.[5] What this uncovered confirmed the extent of the

---

[5] Published by J.A. Bundgaard 'The Excavation of the Athenian Acropolis 1882-1890' Copenhagen 1974. The original drawings were edited from the papers of Georg Kawerau, published with the aid of a grant from the Carlsberg Foundation. The drawings and photographs by Wilhelm Dörpfeld and Georg Kawerau were from the archives of the German Institute at Athens.

Fig. 3 MAJOR FEATURES REVEALED BY THE EXCAVATION OF 1885-90

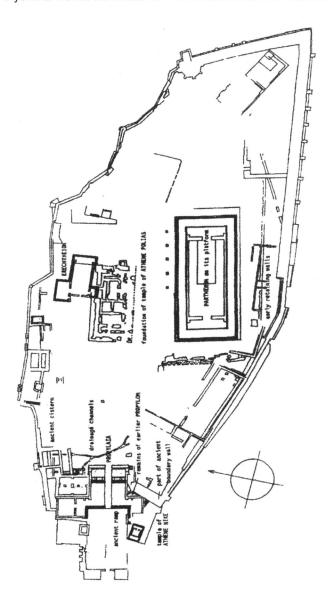

sacrilege committed by the Persians. Numerous vandalised archaic figures of youths and maidens, the hems of whose garments still bore the red colouring to simulate the stitching thread in running patterns of fret, smiling as they did no longer after the holocaust, had been reverently buried just as they were left. Herakles grappling with a sea creature, lions savaging a bull, a triple-bodied demon with tails entwined and smiling heads representing water, fire and earth, had obviously occupied a major temple pediment. A gigantic figure of Athene moving into action, her goatskin aegis bordered with snakes covering her advancing arm, together with falling giants, were all from another pediment estimated to have been 22 metres in length. Many fragments of horsemen and horses, sphinxes, dogs, some modelled in the round, others in relief, as well as sections of smaller pediments belonging to shrines or treasuries, were found beneath the later levels of the ground. These hundreds of pieces of architectural features, of temples, shrines and treasuries large and small, had to be carefully sorted and grouped as belonging to buildings whose purpose and original location could not yet be ascertained. These became known to scholars by the designations A,B,C,D and E given to the groups of pieces by T.Wiegand, based on their supposed architectural relationships.

Many other fragments of stone recovered from the excavation had lettering cut into them. One set of such inscriptions referred to a structure on the Akropolis as the 'Hekatompedon', or the 'hundred-footer', indicating a building of considerable size. As a unit of measurement a Greek foot at the time probably varied slightly from place to place, or even from building to building, but seems to have been greater than the foot measure nowadays of 304.8mm. The architectural fragments of larger scale were now identified with the letter H to associate them with this larger structure of still unknown purpose and unknown location.[6]

Of great significance for the history of the Parthenon was the discovery of the lines of foundation of another large temple set on the rock between the present Erekhtheion and the Parthenon. This foundation had an overall width which corresponded to the 22 metre pediment, home of some of the sculptures of Athene and the giants which had been uncovered.   There existed reference to a 'venerable temple' of Athene, and W.Dörpfeld identified these foundations as belonging to this 'venerable temple' and linked them with the stone elements of entablature built into the north wall of the Akropolis. But what had been the original location of the marble drums also found there, and where had the 'hundred-footer' been located?

It seems to have been forgotten for many years that in 1836 Ross had noted signs of fire damage on the foundation supporting the Parthenon, similar to the thermal fracturing of the marble drums built into the north wall.   This had suggested to Ross that the damage to both was a result of the Persian attack of 480 BC. The Englishman F.C.Penrose, encouraged by Cockerell, had at last been able to make a thorough measurement of the Parthenon in 1846-7.   He agreed with Ross that the immured marble drums and the foundation were both pre-Persian-visit in date and he alone, of all the scholars writing on the subject immediately after the 1885-90 excavations, persisted in this view.   Dörpfeld, Foucart, Kopp and Fürtwangler differed among themselves as to whether the Parthenon foundation was commenced on a variety of dates between 471 and 454 BC.

---

[6] For a discussion of this subject see Dinsmoor 'The Hekatompedon on the Athenian Acropolis' A.J.A.51 1947

Then, in 1902, A.Michaelis drew attention to a literary reference which suggested that as early as 506 BC there had been two temples to Athene on the Akropolis, and he proposed that one of them had been an earlier Erekhtheion. Dörpfeld surveyed the evidence again and rediscovered Ross's notes about the fire damage. This persuaded him that the Parthenon foundation must have been built as early as 506 BC to receive a temple which was built and later destroyed by the Persians, the same foundation which was to provide the site for the Parthenon. Both he and Wiegand believed the 'H' temple had been an archaic structure which had stood on the central part of those foundations discovered between the Erekhtheion and the Parthenon.

Later, further pieces of H scale architectural cornice fragments were identified and more pieces were recovered from a well outside the Akropolis. It became clear that the building they had belonged to would have been too large to fit the inner parts of the temple foundation which had been thought to be its support, and yet too small to fit the width defined by the outer lines of foundation. It was not until 1947 that W.B.Dinsmoor pointed out that the outer lines of foundation had carried a peristyle of pillars around a central naos, and that the pieces of architrave features among the H fragments which came from the flanks of the building were not of a kind which could span beween pillars but needed a solid wall beneath them for their support. Although there are dissenting opinions on the matter, Dinsmoor clarified what had been a puzzling dilemma for at least fifty years. There had been two major temples on the Akropolis. The 'venerable naos' on the site between the Erekhtheion and the Parthenon, the earliest version so old it had figured in Homer's 'Iliad' as the shrine of Athene in the 'house of Erekhtheios', the mythical king of Athens, with it or its successor being replaced around 529 BC by Peisistratos. This temple, destroyed by the

Persians in 480 BC had acquired the name 'venerable' by virtue of its location and its inheritance.   The other, the Hekatompedon, was a temple erected around 566 BC at the inauguration of the four-yearly Panathenaic festival and games. It had strong civic significance, quite separate from that of the ancient and venerable temple alongside.   Dinsmoor concluded that since no other foundation of the requisite size had been uncovered in the systematic excavation of 1885-90, the location of temple H, the Hekatompedon, was under the foundation of the Parthenon itself.   This would explain other references to the Parthenon being known in turn as the Hekatompedon in the same way as the Peisistratid temple of Athene had assumed the name 'venerable' even when it was quite new.

In 488 BC the Athenians had to agree to dismantle the old Hekatompedon and build a new foundation to accommodate the larger marble temple planned as its replacement.   It is this foundation which became the site for the earlier Parthenon started in the 480's, and in turn the support for the later version which can be seen today.

In 1921 Dinsmoor published his revised reconstruction of the building accounts of the Parthenon.   These had been recorded and inscribed annually on the four vertical faces of a stone measuring 1.6 metres high, 1.8 metres wide and 206mm thick, for exhibition to the Athenian citizens.   At that time, 447-432 BC, there had to be such a public display because the funding of the building projects was from Athene's treasury, which by then was under democratic control and scrutiny.   This large stele was eventually shattered into many fragments of varying size which became dispersed, posing a complicated three-dimensional puzzle for later scholars.   Several people attempted to decipher the records these contained from the relatively few pieces

Fig. 4 PLAN OF THE HEKATOMPEDON AS DEFINED BY DINSMOOR   (1947)

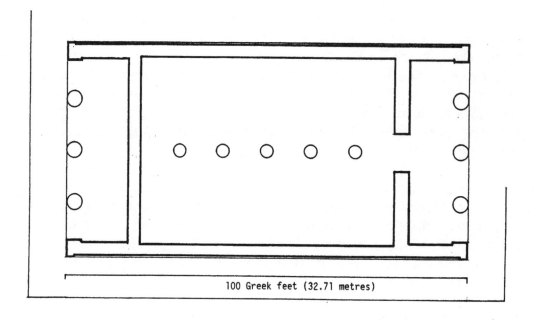

100 Greek feet (32.71 metres)

which were found and identified.   Dinsmoor's reconstruction established the starting and finishing dates for the building of the Parthenon as 448 and 438 BC and these have been widely accepted.

The general belief is that during the thirty years before 448 BC no new work took place on this foundation.[7]   Records of an oath, allegedly sworn before the battle of Plataia in 479 BC, that the holy places destroyed by the Persians should be left as a memorial of their barbarism, have been quoted to supply the reason why this should be, and it has been thought that the apparent paucity of evidence of temple building throughout Attika during those years supports this hypothesis.

It would have been a curious contradiction, an oath which is essentially atheistic; one promising at a time of petition that, out of gratitude for the gods' future help, their ravaged sanctuaries would be left in ruins!   Some theological explanation is required before the genuine nature of such a clause in an oath can be supported.[8]

---

[7] Ranging from Dinsmoor 'The Architecture of Ancient Greece' 1950 p.150 to Parker, 'Athenian Religion' 1996 p.122

[8] The oath before Plataia has survived in two distinct forms.   One of them, a literary record, was a description by the Sicilian historian Diodoros, writing over four hundred years later, sometime between 60 and 30 BC, of how the Greek allies took council together on the Isthmus linking Boeotia and Attika with the Peleponnese and swore: *"I will not set life before liberty, nor will I desert my leaders alive or dead. I will bury all allied troops who die in the battle, and, if I defeat the barbarians in the war, I will not raze to the ground any of the cities that fought against them, and I will not rebuild any temple that has been burnt and destroyed, but I will let them be and leave them as a memorial of the sacrilege of the barbarians"* (Meiggs 'The Athenian Empire' 1972 p 504). There is another similar version which, like that of Diodoros, may derive from Ephoros.   This survived as part of the recorded speech by Lukourgos, an Athenian orator who was prosecuting Leocrates around 330 BC.   His version of the oath contained another clause,   *"and I will tithe all the cities that have sided with the barbarians"*.   This accords in some respects with an oath sworn by Greeks when Xerxes's army was forcing a way through the forests of Macedonia, one quoted by

The archaeological evidence is not so overwhelming as to make it certain that the temple building clause of the oath was both genuine and accepted by all the Greeks who fought at Plataia. The Plataians themselves were certainly not dissuaded from expressing their thanksgiving for the remarkable victory fought on their land.   According to Plutarch,[9] the Plataians were awarded the prize for valour in preference to the rival claims of Spartans and Athenians, and eighty talents of the spoils were used to rebuild the sanctuary of Athene, set up a shrine and decorate the temple with frescoes.   There was no mention of a deferment of this until the signing of a peace with Persia. Perhaps it was some years later that they commissioned Pheidias to erect for them a huge Athene Area, presumably for the sanctuary of that name.   Also, at Phlya below Pentelikon, Themistokles rebuilt the family shrine.   This had been a small hall of Mysteries, the new walls of which he arranged to be painted at his own expense, according to the contemporary poet Simonides.[10]   We know about the little shrine, erected on the banks of the Ilissos to Boreas, the North Wind who had destroyed a Persian fleet, only because Herodotos mentioned it,[11] but there must have been many similar minor dedications erected or restored throughout the region.   The date of rebuilding work at Eleusis, which may be post-Persian, is disputed, but there is major development work on the Akropolis at Athens which is attributed to Kimon in the 460's.

Herodotos(7-132), that when the war was fought to a successful conclusion,*"they would punish all the men of Greek blood who, without compulsion, yielded to the Persians, and dedicate a tenth of their property to the God at Delphi".*

[9] Plutarch 'Aristeides' 20

[10] Plutarch 'Themistokles' 1-4

[11] Herodotos 7-189. This records the second occasion when Boreas, the North Wind, came to the aid of the Athenians against the Persian fleet.   As well as earning the erection of a shrine in his name on the Ilissos, it may also have ensured his portrayal in the metopes of the south flank of the Parthenon, recorded by Carrey.

(2)   Kimon's wall

Hitherto, Kimon's building of the huge south and east walls of the Akropolis has never been satisfactorily explained.   Did Kimon consider that the Akropolis defences were especially weak along these two reaches?   Herodotos's account of how the defences of the Akropolis were breached by the Persians in 480 BC must have been based on Persian sources, since he reported that no Athenian survived the siege.   The main attack was launched against the boarded-up gateway at the west end where a ramped approach had been built in the 6th century to enable large elements of building material to be brought into the sanctuary.   Unlike now, this was then the 'back door' to the site, the 'front' being at the east end, the direction all the major temples faced to greet the rising sun and where, below, lay the greater part of the early city.   A small detachment of Persian mountain troops presumably searched the perimeter wall of the Akropolis for an alternative route into the sanctuary, and it was an unlikely spot which was eventually located, above the Sanctuary of Aglauros at the east end near the south-east corner.   It was so unlikely that the Persians found it to be undefended and were able thereby to enter the Akropolis, no doubt to the dismay of the defenders posted at the west end[12].

Upon retaking their city the Athenians themselves would not have known where the breach had been made; all the corpses would have been found at the west end or within the ruins of the temples. Their earliest immediate attempts to strengthen the defences were concentrated on the north wall, where Themistokles used damaged masonry from the building site of the new Temple of Athene to block up a suspected weakness at

---

[12]. See G. Dontas 1983 'The True Aglaurion' Hesperia 52 48-63

Fig. 5 THEMISTOKLES' ATTEMPT TO SEAL A GAP IN THE NORTH WALL

the spot where another ancient entrance into the 'high city' used to exist on the north side on a line with the planned east front of the new temple. (See figs. 1 and 3) A depression in the ground can still be seen as the site of Themistokles's efforts.

Because the general ground level here was relatively high this new alignment of the north wall did not need to be constructed as a retaining wall and it was built with less thickness than Kimon's later wall along the east and south sides of the Akropolis. (See fig. 3)   The reason for Kimon's enormous expenditure on the south wall was revealed in the excavation of the 1880's.   The temple, which was to celebrate the victory at Marathon, was conceived on a large scale befitting the location on what was to be made the most prominent part of the Akropolis, and also to pay homage to the goddess Athene, patroness of the city, whose help in the battle was to be suitably acknowledged. An essential element of the whole architectural concept was to create an extensive terrace to the south and east of the proposed new temple by raising the ground level.   This is clear from the manner in which the temple podium was built, with solid masonry placed course by course above the natural rock, rising ever higher above the original ground along the south, west and east sides.   It was designed and built from the start with the intention that its external faces would be covered up by later raising the ground level along its south side.   No attempt was made to dress the face of the stone platform as it grew through 17 courses and a height of over 9 metres at the south-east corner.   The faces of adjoining stones were not aligned.   Joints were not close fitting or regular in width, and would have still appeared so were the faces of the stones to be dressed back at a later date.   Only the top four courses were accurately laid with the stones closely fitted.   The third course from the top was featured by dressing around the vertical joints as well as the horizontal ones. Clearly, from the start in the

Fig. 6 SOUTH FACE OF THE FOUNDATION OF THE PARTHENON EXPOSED BY EXCAVATION

early 480's, the plan was that these upper levels alone were intended to be seen, those below were not. If Dinsmoor's dating is accepted, this podium would have been completed at least a year before the Persian army arrived.   By finding Persian fire debris there, Ross established in the 1830's that the ground level next to the podium in 480 BC had already risen to within 4 metres of the top of the foundation.   The raising of the huge south boundary wall of the Akropolis in later years was therefore neither a Kimonian innovation nor a massive defensive investment.   The threat of further attack by the old enemy had faded by the 460's.   Kimon, a friend of Sparta, knew that although Sparta resented the Athenians rebuilding their defensive walls, Spartans would never attack the sanctuary of the gods which all Hellenic people worshipped, so there was no question of erecting the Akropolis walls for defensive purposes. The wall was a necessary part of the original design plan for the temple, a plan put into effect in the 480's, long before any need for defence was recognised.   The south wall was required to be as substantial as it is in order to hold back the vast amount of waste material and other types of fill which would be required to cover the rough masonry of most of the podium faces and eventually support a terrace around the southern side of the temple.   In the early years, before 480, the dumped earth and fill material adjacent to the temple was held back by an ancient retaining wall, (wall 2 on fig. 7) made with polygonal masonry. Its presence and the polygonal technique used in its construction, similar to that supporting the edge of the 6th century approach ramp at the west end suggest it was erected to perform the same task during the building of the earlier Hekatompedon on its smaller platform foundation on the same site.   Later, while work on Kimon's huge wall was starting, a slender second, relief retaining wall, (wall 3 on fig. 7) was built

31

Fig. 7 MADE-UP GROUND SOUTH OF THE PARTHENON, BASED ON DÖRPFELD 1902

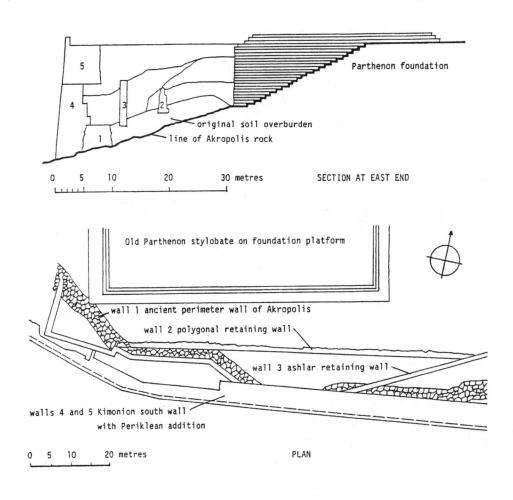

Parthenon foundation

original soil overburden

line of Akropolis rock

0   5   10   20   30 metres   SECTION AT EAST END

Old Parthenon stylobate on foundation platform

wall 1 ancient perimeter wall of Akropolis

wall 2 polygonal retaining wall

wall 3 ashlar retaining wall

walls 4 and 5 Kimonion south wall
    with Periklean addition

0   5   10   20 metres   PLAN

some distance down the slope, presumably to protect workmen building the main south wall below.   Without a proper foundation, being on made-up ground, this was clearly a temporary precautionary structure.

It is conservatively estimated that 15-18,000m³, of dressed stone, equal to over 5,000 wagon loads, were needed to build Kimon's part of the south wall.   This was a major construction in itself but the stone was the smaller part of the material needed inside the sanctuary in order to raise the terrace.   Access to the building work on the wall for labourers manhandling the stone required the ground level behind to be raised in step with the masonry.   The purpose of the wall was to enlarge the usable area of the Akropolis site, and the wall's function was to hold back the earth which would support the future terrace, so it made sense to keep the two processes in step with one another. Thousands of cubic metres of fill were required, the main sources of which lay outside the sanctuary.   In the early years after the Persian holocaust, the debris left by them would have provided much of the fill material needed on the Akropolis.   A computer-simulated assessment of the volume of fill above natural ground levels to the top of the Kimonian section of the south and east walls would indicate the actual scale of this work.   In the absence of this, a sample area lying between the temple podium, 76.9m long, and the south wall, can illustrate the point. Dörpfeld drew two sections through this area in 1902, based on the excavation in the 1880's, and they show that this length of wall alone would have retained up to 8,000m³, during the period of the 460's.   The length of the Kimonian wall was about 370m, possibly retaining 35,000m³, of fill.   This would have been most efficiently carried by individual pack mules; 200 mules could have done it in 3 years, allowing for the many days of festival.

It is easy to see how Kimon's wall became part of the early 5th century folklore of Athens, rather than the temple itself, which was its reason for existence; the building of the wall was a colossal enterprise, employing many hundreds of men, beasts and wagons, and to the eye of the common man, the extra effort involved in the building of the temple would have appeared puny in comparison. The real significance of the south wall of the Akropolis, built in the 460's, is its testimony that the idea of building the Temple of Athene to celebrate Marathon had not been abandoned. Immediately after the departure of the Persians there had been far more urgent priorities for the people of Attika.

Quite apart from taking back, resettling and replanting the land from which they had farmed no crops for two whole years, they had been involved in annual military campaigns against the retreating Persians around the coast of Ionia, Caria, Lycia and among the Dodecanese islands until 467 BC, taking a leading part, with Aristeides as their main representative, in setting up the Delian alliance to prosecute the war, dealing with minor and major revolts among the allies and with the deep suspicions of the Spartans. In addition, the Athenian builders had to reconstruct their shattered city with its defensive walls, its essential civic buildings and the houses of its people, all destroyed by the retreating Persian army. Themistokles had persuaded his fellow citizens to build a complete new harbour at Peiraieus and start the development of a new town behind it. Substantial walls were erected around the new port and, later, long walls were set up to connect it with Athens itself. If there had been any notion in 479 to leave the wrecked sanctuary on the Akropolis until there was time to deal with it, or to keep it as a memorial of barbarism, the evidence of the re-alignment and rebuilding of its south wall confirms that by 467 BC there was a change in the mind of Kimon and his friends, and therefore of many other Athenians who also admired him, towards a more positive view of Athenian supremacy.   This manifested itself in a costly determination to celebrate not only the heroism of their fathers in the 480's, but also their own more recent and decisive victories as well.   It is difficult to believe that all this expenditure of effort and money was committed to the massive south wall and the terrace without work on the earlier Parthenon being resumed at the same time.   New marble would need to be delivered from the quarry to replace that damaged by the Persians, and doubtless there would have been marble blocks intended for the temple stock-piled in the quarry during the months when the invaders were approaching Athens, stone which would have to be moved to allow the quarry to resume production for other projects as well as the temple.

The absence of contemporary epigraphic evidence of the commissioning of the earlier Parthenon and of Kimon's building activity on the Akropolis is not surprising if the work was being promoted, until Ephialtes's democratic reforms of 461 BC, by the leadership of the aristocratic Areopagos, who were still likely to take such initiatives without much prior reference to the demos and funded, probably to a large degree, by individual contributions made by the wealthier citizens.   Much of this would have included help in the form of gifted slave labour, of which there would have been no shortage after the successful military campaigns which had been fought.   In Kimon's day there would have been little strain put upon the Athenian economy by the resumption of the project to build a temple of thanksgiving dedicated to Athene, including all the necessary related works associated with it.   It is not inconceivable that it would have been seen as a useful outlet for the windfall of slave energy resulting from the success of the Athenian military campaigns.   The building activity certainly gained for Kimon political backing of two kinds; from his aristocratic friends, who recognised the power component which accompanied it, and also from the hundreds of Athenian small contractors, skilled artisans and traders whose economic well-being was temporarily boosted by the enterprise. Perikles, a newcomer to the political scene at this time must have learned much by observing the way in which political support could be purchased by promoting a project so rich in employment for the citizens of Athens, citizens who were potential supporters of his own democratic aims.

STUDY 2   BUILDING THE PARTHENON.

Before the relationship between the earlier Parthenon conceived in the 480's and the Parthenon which was built in the 440's can be examined, it is necessary to understand how the huge elements of their structure, so alike in form and scale, were shaped and assembled.   Some processes of that shaping had to be worked at ground level while others could only be carried out on the stones after they were placed.   The methods used to assemble the elements and the order of erection, which was dictated both by the scale of the parts and the nature of the hoisting tackle required for the task, will be seen to be important factors in understanding that relationship.   Most of the clues to the discovery of how the two Parthenons were built lie in the publication by Penrose of the measurements of the ruins of the later temple which he made in 1846-7.[1]   These clues to the construction system employed emerge almost as a by-product of Penrose's studies because his main interest lay in recording the subtleties of profile of the elements of the architecture rather than in any systematic work on the techniques of construction used.   As a result, he did not always interpret correctly the structural implications of what he recorded.[2]

In 488 BC the architects were embarking on a novel enterprise - to build an extraordinarily large temple, every visible element of whose structure was, for the first time, to be composed of Pentelic marble.   This exquisite material, which had hitherto been used for relatively minor works and sculptural pieces, had to be won from a quarry nearly eighteen kilometres north of Athens and transported to the Athenian Akropolis, a rocky

---

[1] 'An Investigation of the Principles of Athenian Architecture, or, The results of a survey conducted chiefly with reference to the optical refinements exhibited in the construction of the ancient buildings at Athens.' 1851 2nd edition 1888
[2] Examples are given later in the text and in note 2.19.

outcrop some eighty metres above the surrounding plain. Many temples had been built before the Parthenon, and many more were built later, using coarser material found locally, building stone which, while being worked to standards of great precision, relied on an applied final stucco finish to produce the monolithic effect the architects of the time sought.   In this new temple for Athene, in the city which took its name from her, the attempt was made to build with such precision and accuracy that, without resort to the use of a stucco skin, the joints between the stones would not be apparent. There was no precedent for such a procedure on this scale; so how was this achieved and, in particular, how were the major elements - the perimeter pillars - made to appear to be identical with one another while being fashioned by large numbers of masons? Their work had to stand scrutiny without relying on any later processes of covering up.

(1)   The controlling role of the architects

Apart from Penrose's measurements, which provide the most detailed information to answer these questions, two ancient documents survive which establish that important building operations were conducted in accordance with designs made by architects and that every stage of the erection process was supervised by an architect's representative on the site.[3] One of these records related to the enlargement of the Hall of Mysteries at Eleusis and the other to the building of an arsenal at Peiraieus, each document representing a different stage in the process organised by the architect responsible for the works. The arsenal document was a general description of the building in words, with the main dimensions stated, the kind of document used to invite tenders for carrying out parts of the contract.   It

---

[3] IG2· 1668 and 1666.   The texts with translations and notes are given in Bundgaard's 'Mnesicles' 1957.

was made clear that dimensioned details would be supplied by the architect at the appropriate time so that the contractors knew they would not be expected to budget for the supply of such details themselves.

The inscription for the work at Eleusis was an order list for stone from several sources.   The stone from Aigina was intended for use as ashlar blocks and for triglyphs.   Precise sizes were given for estimating the cost of the quarrying, the hauling and the final shaping stages, and the price had to include setting the stones in position and securing them with clamps and dowels surrounded with molten lead wherever the architect directed.   Such details of structural security were not left to the mason, and the implication was that the architect's representative would inspect each course of stone laid.   Stones for the cornice and the metopes at Eleusis had to be obtained from the quarry on Mount Pentelikon, with overall sizes being defined on the order list, where it was also stated that further specifications as to shape, location and detailed finishing would be supplied by the architect.   Clearly these documents were prepared and issued by him. Neither of them could have been written without preliminary layout drawings being made and carefully dimensioned by the people who organised the entire procedure. The architect would have drawn the overall arrangements of the work to scale, with calculated dimensions added, just as he does today.   He would have used assembled boards of wood with the grain filled and whitened as a surface to draw upon with lead. Similar wooden boards that 5th century Athenian painters used for the large pictorial representations of their ancestors' past glories, exhibited in the Painted Stoa, were seen by Pausanias six hundred years later, so they must have been expertly prepared. By the mid-century it was evidently a well established procedure. From these drawings on wood the architect had to prepare others which were useful to the craftsmen.

Until the discovery by Lothar Haselberger of the drawings incised on the unfinished walls of the Temple of Apollo at Didyma,[4] there was some speculation about how an ancient Greek architect's instructions were conveyed to the workmen.   Much of this had degenerated into a mythology that drawings were not in fact needed, that the Greek craftsmen were so skilled that somehow, by calculation alone, a complete building could be brought into being by the collective efforts of the workmen on the site.   Such a view ignores the reality that, for an enterprise of this nature, large numbers of workmen would need the detailed directions of a creative intelligence and a co-ordinating mind able to establish a procedure which all the teams of masons could follow.   This was the only way of ensuring that their efforts would have uniform results.

The drawings at Didyma show that there the architect's instructions were drawn by him on a wall.   In the case of the Parthenon they were probably drawn on the peristyle pavement, since the walls would not be there while the first pillars were being erected along the west, south and north sides. (The reason for this is explained below on p.75 and fig.25)   The architect's outlines were then lightly drafted into the stone and the marks used to define the shapes of all the parts.   From these the teams of masons, using adjustable dividers, took their required measurements to the stones they were working on.   The fact that the Temple of Apollo at Didyma was never completed has preserved the faintly incised drawings, since the final procedure of rubbing down and smoothing all the wall surfaces would have erased them. No original drawings of the Parthenon remain. This does not mean the temple was built without them but that the working drawings were removed during the finishing of the stonework. The Greek builders recognised that working draw-

---

[4] 'Scientific American' December 1984 p.114-122.

Fig. 8 DRAWINGS DISCOVERED ON THE WALLS OF THE TEMPLE OF APOLLO AT
DIDYMA BY L. HASELBERGER

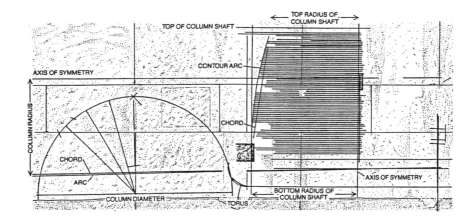

PENROSE'S PLATE 14

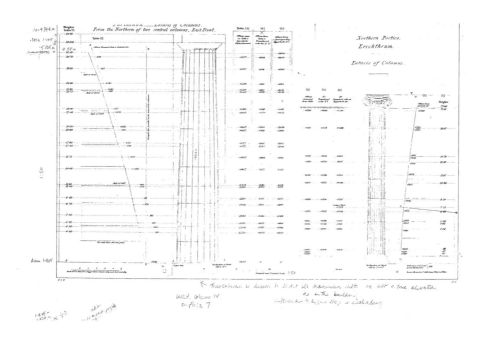

Fig 9 PAVEMENT LEVELS IN MILLIMETRES BELOW HIGHEST POINTS MARKED AS "datum" DERIVED FROM PENROSE PLATES 10, 11, 12 AND 13 WITH PHOTOGRAPHS OF UPWARD CURVE ON STYLOBATE

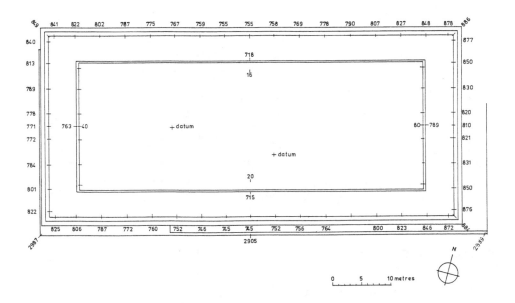

East front stylobate curve

South edge of base to earlier Parthenon

ings were merely a means of communication and could serve no further purpose once the building was complete.   Design drawings were no doubt useful then, as they are now, in educating others in the art, by comparing drawings with the finished building, but that was a private activity.

The outlines of every moulding would have been drawn at full size (some of these survive at Didyma) from which patterns would be made for the use of the masons working on those parts of the fabric which had to be finished before being lifted into position on the temple - parts such as the overhanging cornice stones, the triglyphs, metopes, most of the shaped sections of the architrave beams and any undercut details which would be otherwise inaccessible for further finishing work once the stone was placed in situ.   These profiles would be the result of many studies of what had been built before, as well, no doubt, as many rejected alternatives for what was now to be translated into stone.   Many of these studies carried out by the architect had to be made, even before the size of the stylobate base could be determined, as the details of the pillars and their relationship to the edge of the top step governed the overall dimensions.

(2) The effect of the vertical curve given to the stylobate

Penrose's measurements on his plates 10,11,12 and 13 show by how much the stylobate platform was deliberately made to rise towards the centre in a very flat, dome-shaped curve.   This information, translated into metric measure, is summarised on Fig.9 which also shows that the upward curve on the top surface of the platform is not so pronounced as that on the Parthenon stylobate itself.   The domed surface formed on the stylobate meant that each pillar had to stand on a slightly sloping base and, moreover, the direction of the slope was different for each pillar.   Penrose's Plates 7 and 8 (see figs. 35 and 36) reveal[5] that the pillars were made to lean inwards. The accommodation of the slope of the stylobate - slightly different for each pillar which stood upon it - and the imparting of the lean to the pillar in another direction, was achieved in the shaping of the top and bottom surfaces of the lowest drum.   At the time the pillars were set out, the stylobate upper surface had been dressed to the slightly domed shape, but was still some 10mm above the intended final surface. This can be seen on the surviving stylobate stones from the earlier Parthenon.[6]   The 10mm mantle was to protect the pavement while all the building work was in progress above.   Only at the end of the work would the pavement marble be reduced to its final surface.   At this early stage the pillar locations were marked out, in the case of the Parthenon started in 447 BC, centred on joints between the large stones of the stylobate.   A shallow circular sinking was cut down to the final platform surface to receive the lowest drum of the pillar.   Because the surface of the platform was everywhere sloping in slightly different compass directions, a feature resulting from its domed form, the alignment of the maximum slope on this flat bottomed, but not level, sinking had to be found, and its relation to the joint between the stylobate stones had to be measured where it met the circumference of the pillar bottom.

Three instruments which the masons and the site architect used regularly were required for this critical stage. These were a right-angled frame, adjustable dividers with metal pins at the tips for accurately measuring and transferring dimensions from a full-

[5] See Study 3.1 and figures 35 and 36 .
[6] See B.H.Hill 'The Older Parthenon' A.J.A.16 1912, figure 11 - reproduced here as figure 56.

size drawing to the stone being worked, and a gravity level.[7]
The common form of this level was an isosceles triangle made of
wood, with a plumb-line suspended from the apex.   When the
base of the triangle was placed on a stone, the plumb-line
aligned with a marked centre line of the base, if the stone surface
was horizontal.   Placed on a straight-edge at least equal in
length to the diameter of a round pillar stone, a wedge-shaped
measure inserted between the edge of the stone and the straight-
edge would show by how much the stone was not horizontal and
indicate how much material had to be cut away at the other end
to achieve horizontality. This was the kind of practical information a mason needed; angles of slope were meaningless to him.
A well equipped architect would have had a refined version of
this form of level, one so dimensioned, with the overall height
equal to the length of the base, that the plumb-bob would
register, on a scale inscribed on the base of the triangle, by how
much a true flat surface was out of level in relation to the known
length of the base.   Sockets cast in bronze for each of the special
angles of this triangle would allow different sets of wooden
spacers to make up triangles of the required dimensions for each
particular application.

(3)   The shape of the pillar drums

When it came to defining how the pillar drums were shaped and
then assembled, even Penrose was deceived by some of the
unfinished stones discovered on the site during the excavation of
1885-90, and Bundgaard, who also attempted to explain how

---

[7] See J-P Adam 'Roman Building' ch. 2c.

Fig. 10 FINDING THE DIRECTION OF MAXIMUM SLOPE ON THE STYLOBATE

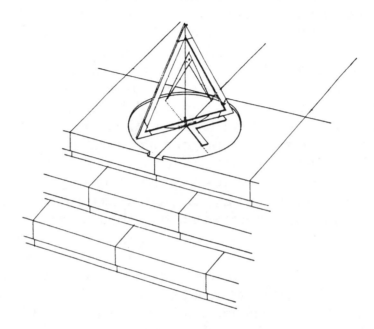

Fig 11 ARCHITECT'S GRAVITY LEVEL AND WORKMAN'S VERSION

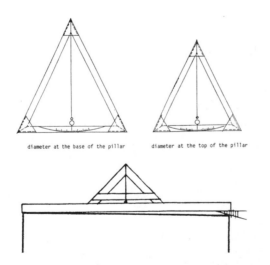

diameter at the base of the pillar   diameter at the top of the pillar

pillars were made, was similarly misled.[8]   The making of pillars passed through a stage described in the accounts for the building of the Erekhtheion as "unsmoothed and unribbed", in other words, with a mantle of stone left around them just as the pavement stones were left while other work proceeded above. Penrose described the form of the pillars at this stage as being "cylindrical or, more correctly, of a conical shape".   Base drums, recorded by Penrose, uncovered in the excavation of the Akropolis site in the 1880's, were seen to be conical, slightly smaller in diameter at the top than at the bottom, leading Bundgaard to assume that each stone drum was worked in this way.   When he came to explain how the entasis - the outward-swelling curve given to the taper on the pillar - was achieved, he was led towards a fantasy of full-size wooden profiles, thirty feet long, being used by the masons as guides.   Penrose had not enquired too closely how the entasis might have been formed although he had measured it accurately.[9]   Dinsmoor was simply overawed by it, and betrayed his misunderstanding of how it was achieved by exclaiming that the work displayed "a mathematical precision which is almost incredible".[10]   Perhaps he was misled also by what remains of the gigantic GT temple at Selinous, to which he gave a date of 520-450 BC., where collapsed pillar drums in various stages of finish reveal attempts to establish a method which resulted in only one pillar being completed, suggesting that the procedure was experimental.   It is not possible to assess how successful the method was, since the pillar is not standing.   Drums of other pillars are faceted and others left with wide fillets between shallow flutes.   It is not known whether entasis was being attempted, a relevant factor since, without entasis, pillar drums could be made conical.

[8] 'Mnesicles' 1957 p.133-140.
[9] See his plate 14, fig.8
[10] 'The Architecture of Ancient Greece' 1950 p.173.

Fig. 12 PENROSE SKETCH OF PILLAR DRUMS EXCAVATED

Partly worked pillar drums discarded, buried and later found in excavations

It is clear that to impart a curved entasis on a pillar, the diameter of the stone midway between the joints must always be greater than the mean between the diameters at top and bottom of each drum.   Accepting conical forms for each drum and for the pillar as a whole makes impossible the achievement of perfect entasis on every arris on every pillar, with each pillar being made identical with the rest.   The unfinished conical base stones found on the Akropolis must have been abandoned as useless, some because of discovered faults in the stone, some because they were damaged, others being false starts made by enthusiastic but undisciplined masons who had still to learn how to set about the task.   The last temple of comparable size in Athens, the Temple of Athene Polias on the Akropolis, had been finished at least twenty-five years before the teams of masons were assembled to learn how to build the earlier Parthenon with the unforgiving material Pentelic marble.

(4)   How the pillars were made to lean inwards

The details recorded by Penrose suggest that the method of achieving the intended result would have had to be as follows. The bottom drum of the pillar was fashioned into a perfect cylinder, with the upper and lower surfaces parallel with one another and at right angles to the curved surface.   The diameter was made equal to the overall base diameter required for the pillar, plus an allowance all around which was the protective mantle.   On to the upturned base of this stone were drawn out the twenty scallop shapes called flutes, but initially only a few centimetres of these flutes were cut down into the drum and the mantle removed.   Several such stones belonging to the earlier Parthenon were found with only this amount of work carried out. One of the flutes was selected as that to be facing the edge of the stylobate, and the direction of the maximum slope of the stylobate at the location selected for the pillar was transferred to

Fig. 13 THE BASE STONE UPTURNED FOR CUTTING THE FLUTES

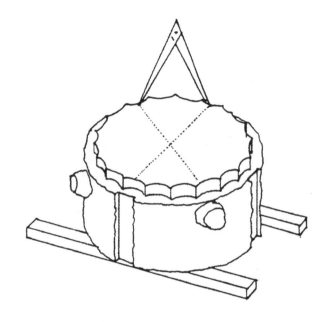

the upturned drum in correct relationship to it.   Along this line stone was cut away, at one end to the depth indicated by the gravity level reading, and tapering evenly to nought at the other end.   The whole surface of this scallop edged shape was made true to this slope, ensuring that when the stone was turned over and lowered into the sinking cut in the stylobate, the two sloping surfaces of the pavement and the bottom of the lowest drum would come together to make the upper surface of the drum horizontal.

This top surface had next to be worked to a slope which would induce a lean to the pillar above.   Knowing the intended height of the pillar from the scaled and dimensioned drawings prepared by the architect, knowing also the diameter of the pillar at the base and how much the pillar was to lean inwards at the top, simple proportional ratios indicated how much stone, (x), had to be removed from the rear of the drum's top surface for the desired result. $x = LD/H$ where H=height, D=diameter, L =lean.

The upper surface of this lowest drum was now no longer a true circle, so a new centre had to be established and marked.   On the Parthenon none of the pillars were made up of regular and equal courses, and this is where the architect's working drawing of the outline of the whole pillar became necessary.   Because the pillar shafts were to be identical with each other, and yet made up of irregular heights of stone, a standard outline of a pillar was required which would apply to all of them.   Only the radius at top and bottom of each stone drum was of interest to the masons at this stage, so one diagram, with the horizontal dimensions drawn to their full size, could serve for two pillars. (See fig.15) The architect would have had the template for the pillar profile made with the height reduced to a quarter of its full size, thus exaggerating its curvature, but showing the diameter at top and

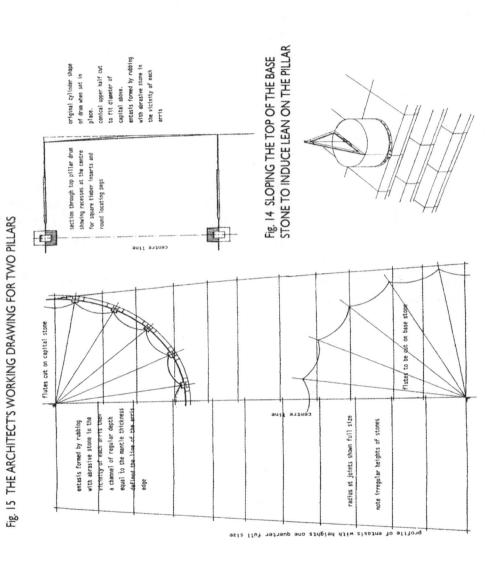

Fig. 15 THE ARCHITECT'S WORKING DRAWING FOR TWO PILLARS

original cylinder shape
of drum when set in
place.

conical upper half cut
to fit diameter of
capital above.

entasis formed by rubbing
with abrasive stone in
the vicinity of each
arris

section through top pillar drum
showing recesses at the centre
for square timber inserts and
round locating pegs

centre line

Fig. 14 SLOPING THE TOP OF THE BASE
STONE TO INDUCE LEAN ON THE PILLAR

flutes cut on capital stone

entasis formed by rubbing
with abrasive stone in the
vicinity of each arris then
a channel of regular depth
equal to the mantle thickness
defined the line of the arris
edge

centre line

radius at joints shown full size

note irregular heights of stones

flutes to be cut on base stone

profile of entasis with heights one quarter full size

bottom at the correct dimensions (about 2.4metres would thus represent the height of the pillar and about 1.95 metres its width at the base including an allowance for the mantle).   A template would have been one of those useful models devised for a specific task on a particular building and kept for reference purposes. The mason could see the product resulting from it and could use it again, either directly or modified to bring about whatever refinement he wished.   With other moulding profiles made of timber, these were both the means of perpetuating a traditional way of working and the basis for making changes in design.   The entasis template for the earlier Parthenon, for instance, may have been a variation of that used on the final four pillars at the Temple of Aphaia on Aigina, which were also made up of drums of stone (the others were monoliths).   Aigina was only 15 miles away from the ancient Athens port of Phaleron and the Temple of Aphaia had been completed only a few years before designs were being prepared for the earlier Parthenon.   The architect of the earlier Parthenon could have had access to the templates used there and, knowing how the pillars produced from them had turned out, he could readily make any modifications he wished to arrive at the outline of those he was designing.   The overall pillar heights are closely related, those at Aigina being 5.272m, almost exactly half the height of those on the later Parthenon, 10.433m, so allowing for the differing proportionate heights of the capitals, the actual timber profiles used for the pillar outlines of each temple could have been of identical length.

To make the diagram for the use of the masons working on the pillars, a centre line was scratched on the pavement and, on either side of it and spaced from it by the radius of the pillar at the base and at the top, the foreshortened curve of the swelling entasis was marked.   Each team of masons assigned to make and erect the drums for a particular pillar used one half of such a diagram to record the final height of each stone, after laying it

Fig. 16 FINDING THE NEW CENTRE FOR THE TOP SURFACE

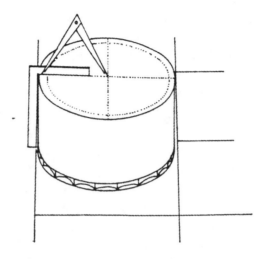

Fig. 17 THE BASE READY TO RECEIVE THE NEXT DRUM

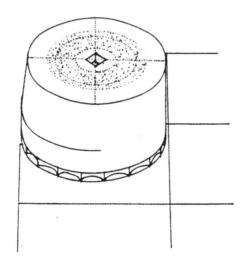

and preparing the top surface to receive the next.   The line they made on the diagram to record the height (divided by four) of the stone just laid indicated the radius required for the lower surface of the next stone drum. The recording of the height of the first drum laid, showed also the radius to be used to find the new centre for the top surface, which was yet to be restored to a true circular shape.   By the use of a plumb-line at the front and rear of the bottom drum, a centre line was drawn vertically over the centre of the flutes cut into the bottom surface.   A right-angle frame applied along this centre line showed the amount of stone to be removed at the front to make a right angle between the new top surface and the front face.   A radius set in by this amount from the front gave the new centre for the top surface of the drum.

A circumference drawn around this centre showed the amount of stone to be cut away on a taper to nought half way down the drum.   The centre at the top surface was now displaced from the centre of the bedding surface by an amount equal to that required to produce the lean on the pillar.   Next, a square sinking was made around this centre point to receive a wooden block with a hole in it to take a strong dowel projecting to connect first of all with the centre of the grinding stone, and later with the recessed timber block let into the next drum of stone.[11]

(5)   How the stones were joined

Penrose had supposed that as one stone drum was mounted on the one below, it was rotated to grind away any minor irregular-ities left by the masons on the two surfaces which met at the joint.   Perhaps he underestimated the force required to bring

---

[11] In Penrose's day one of these dowel pins from the Propylaia was preserved in the Museum of the Institute of British Architects.   It resembled olive wood but was described as *"juniper cedar"*.

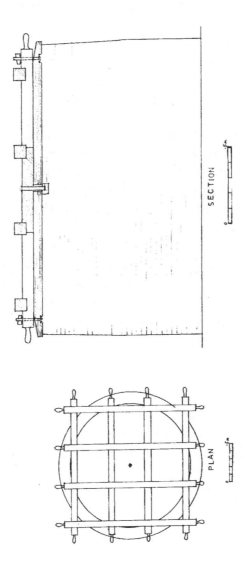

Fig. 18 SURFACE PLATE IDENTIFIED BY M. KORRES. Modified for use as a grinding plate.

this about. Manolis Korres[12] has identified a fragment of stone now in the Akropolis Museum, belonging to a thin disc, equal in diameter to that required to fit the top surface of the largest corner pillar base stone.[13] This 63mm thick fragment is dressed on the top face and pierced in such a way as to suggest that it was originally fastened to a frame-work of timber. Dr. Korres has described it as a surface plate for coating in red colour to indicate high spots on the meeting faces of pillar stones. If the stone fragment was originally abrasive and harder than Pentelic marble, then it could equally well have been a grinding stone fastened, as he suggested, to a frame with sixteen protruding handle grips. These would have enabled the grinding team to lift the grindstone over the marble drum and engage at the centre with the dowel. Then by walking around the stone drum and pushing on the handles, a team of eight men could grind away any slight irregularities of surface on the contact face of the marble. The masons had reduced the contact zone to circular areas at the centre and the perimeter, slightly lowering the area between by roughening it. A perfect fit with the next stone would be ensured by complete circumferences being walked by the team on this stone, and on the lower surface of the next stone being prepared by the masons.

(6)   How the entasis was produced on the pillar profile

From then on upwards, all the stones were cut initially as true cylinders with top and bottom surfaces parallel to one another. The top surface of each new stone was marked off with a circumference indicated by and measured from the pavement

---

[12] 'From Pentelicon to the Parthenon' 1995 figs. 31 and 32.

[13] This is a good example of how the Athenian builders of the time conserved their energy. The stone would be too small for the base diameter of the corner pillars, where it was not required, and it is no larger than it needs to be to fit the reduced upper diameter of the same stones, the largest surfaces upon which it would be used.

Fig. 19 THE PILLAR WITH FOUR DRUMS IN PLACE

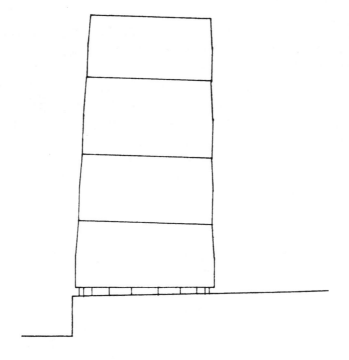

diagram and the surplus stone was cut away to half way down the drum.   As it was assembled, the outline of the whole pillar at that stage would have waved slightly in and out throughout its height, swelling a few millimetres at the mid height of each stone. On the lines joining the arrises at the base with those at the capital, a process of rubbing was next employed to reduce these high spots, not to an even taper, but to an evenly developed gentle curve assessed by the masons' eyes using a straight-edge of timber, possibly 2m long, held in his hand vertically against the line of the future arris.   No material had to be removed in the vicinity of the joints, which were the true dimensional markers along the required surface.   And only 7 or 8mm needed to be rubbed away from the highest spots midway between the joints.   The line of each arris on the pillar had to be established in this way by rubbing with an abrasive stone, being checked for sweetness of line against the straight edge and trimmed again until a perfect flow of continuously curving surface was produced over the full height, but only in the vicinity of each arris -a strip 10cms wide would have been enough.[14]   This surface of course was not the finished one but one a mantle thickness away from the final arris between the flutes yet to be exposed, and all the masons worked to the same specified thickness of mantle.   In this way all the pillars could be produced to look the same as their neighbours.

(7)   How the sloping pavement affected the architrave beams.

The stylobate curving slightly upward towards the centre of the façade, and all the pillars being made approximately the same

---

[14] Another example of Athenian economy of effort.   Others have been uncovered near the Propylaia, where no more of the older Propylon was cut away than was necessary to allow the building of Mnesikles's gateways, thus happily preserving evidence of the forms of that earlier structure within 75mm of the later one.

Fig. 20 VARIATION OF ABACUS HEIGHT

overall height, meant that the architrave beams carried by the pillar capitals had to arch upward in a similar fashion. The arching of the architrave was nearly but not exactly a replica of that of the stylobate below. Some slight move towards the restoration of an apparent horizontality to the tympanum shelf supporting the sculpture was achieved by varying the height of the pillars along the east front, making those at the centre between 10 and 11mm shorter than those at the end of the row.

The arching of the architrave transmitted to the adjacent beams around the corner a soffit plane which sloped in the same direction as the slope on the pavement below. This made the setting of the pillar capitals the most complicated task. Like the majority of the pillar stones, they were made with the top surface parallel with the bedding face. However, the top surface of the capital had to support the architrave beams and therefore needed to slope not inwards, like the joints of all the drums supporting it, but outwards. So the top surface of the last plain drum of the pillar had to be checked for total height above the pavement and, if necessary, corrected and then cut to a slope which would set the capital stone at the appropriate angle to carry the beams and set them to appear to echo the line of the stylobate below. Penrose's fig.3 illustrated this in an exaggerated way. The actual inclinations may be of interest as they reveal the degree of subtlety sought by the designers of the Parthenon. The slope on the pavement in the east-west direction in the middle of the east front is 12mm across the width of the pillar, which is 1.905m. On the lowest drum of the nearest pillar the height above the pavement at the front, near the step, is 28mm greater than the height at the rear of the pillar. This means that the masons worked a slope across the top surface of the lowest drum of 16mm. This is the amount

Fig. 21 PENROSE'S SKETCH SHOWING (EXAGGERATED) SLOPES ON THE BASE
         AND THE TOP DRUMS

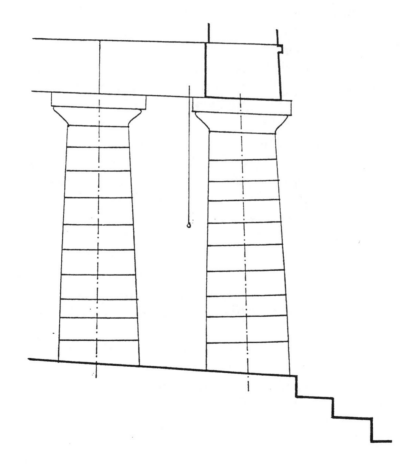

which would have registered on the architect's gravity level scale, and a record of this would have been made on the mantle of the drum so that, using the gravity level, each stone placed above could be checked for correct slope by referring to it. Because all the pillars were made up of drums of random heights, there was no possibility of sighting through, as can be done with a horizontal course in a wall to check that the top surfaces were all at the same slope on each pillar along the front or the flank of the temple. The shaping of the top drum had to convert this slope, inherited from the base stone, to an inclination in the opposite direction to tilt the capital to the proper slope to receive the beams of the architrave - some 5mm out of horizontal across the width of the abacus, back to front of the pillars.

(8)   The technique for finishing the pillars

Only when all the work above the pillars was complete could the finishing of the pillars themselves be carried out. The bottom few centimetres of the lowest drum and the capital stones had already been worked to the scalloped or fluted shape which the rest of the pillar was to receive. A length of twine rubbed in coloured chalk was stretched tightly from the arris at the capital to the corresponding arris at the base and then pulled out and released, as on a bow, to make a mark on the mantle stone. Using this line as a centre guide, a channel was then carefully cut to a regular depth equal to the agreed mantle thickness, possibly about 20mm. This would conform to a tee-shaped gauge which all the masons selected for this crucial task would carry, every gauge being made the same as the rest. When all twenty channels were cut to the true depth and throughout the height of the pillar, the chalked twine was applied again to indicate the final line of the arris on the finished surface. The surplus stone was then cut away and the flutes formed between the arrises to a profile started at the base of the pillar. The later

Fig. 22 THE WHOLE PILLAR WITH CHANNELS CUT PRIOR TO FORMING THE FLUTES

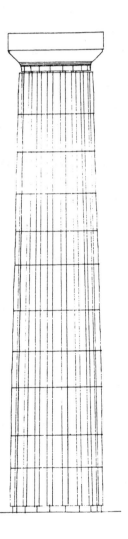

stages were worked by rubbing with a rounded piece of grinding stone and finished with a polishing powder to remove any minor scratch marks.

Writing about the entasis, Penrose reported, "*The edges of the flutes in those columns which had been best preserved from injury, were found to have more regularity of curvature than any profiles which could be obtained within the channels and moreover to be themselves generally somewhat more regular on the outside of the temple than on the inside towards the cella walls, which parts being usually in shade, did not demand the same absolute precision as those where the slightest defect would be made visible by the cast shadow.*"   This shows that in a team of masons collectively building a pillar, the more skilled, and those with the keenest eye, were selected for work where those qualities were most necessary.[15]

(9)   The aesthetic purpose of the flutes on the pillars

The origin of the fluted form of pillar is not securely known. Many-faceted stone pillars dating from the 12th dynasty can be seen at Beni Hasan on the Nile.   It has been suggested by A.W.Lawrence[16] that the form derives from pillars fashioned out of tree trunks, the bark having been cleaned off with a round bladed adze and the effect being found attractive enough to be perpetuated in stone.

But the subtlety of the flutes intended for the Parthenon makes it clear that it was no longer only tradition which preserved the

---

[15] The number of men forming such a team may have varied.   The accounts for the finishing of the Erekhtheion pillars, which were much smaller, give the names of 4,7,6 and 5 men working on the four individual pillars.   The teams were made up of citizens, metics and slaves working together.
[16] 'Greek Architecture' 1957 p.101.

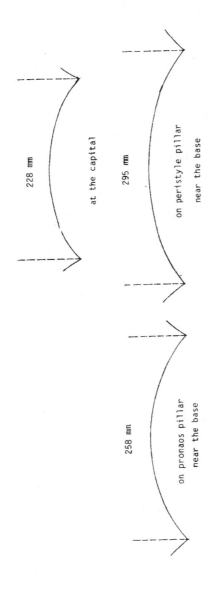

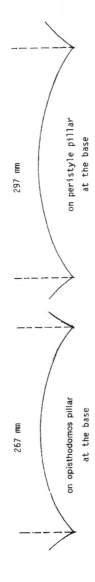

Fig. 23 PROFILES OF FLUTES ON THE PARTHENON

228 mm

at the capital

295 mm

on peristyle pillar
near the base

258 mm

on pronaos pillar
near the base

Profiles of flutes on the earlier Parthenon

297 mm

on peristyle pillar
at the base

267 mm

on opisthodomos pillar
at the base

form.   Cutting flutes into a pillar had always made it stand out against the wall behind and the play of light on them was seen to emphasise the pillar's roundness.   The aesthetic value of it was clearly understood by the architect of the earlier Parthenon started before 480 BC, as can be seen by the profiles of the flutes from that temple which were recorded by Penrose.   On his plate 21 fig.15, he drew the outline of the flute on the Parthenon capital and, on plate 46 fig.3, no.1 (see fig.23), the flute formed on the base stones damaged by the Persians and afterwards built into the north wall of the Akropolis.   Both consist of a flatter segmental curve at the centre and smaller radius curves near the arris.   This tightening of the curve at the edge served to emphasise the dramatic effect of shadows cast by sunlight, sharpening the moment when the shadow appeared, as added percussion can underline a musical note, and prolonging the firmness of the shadow's edge within the flute until the instant the whole flute was cast into shade.   This was a conscious harnessing of an everyday cosmic phenomenon, the visual expression of time passing, making it register with maximum clarity on the man-made forms, measuring the moving shadows out upon the curved and undulating surface.   It was an entirely appropriate development to make for a temple building.

Penrose always analysed the curves on the moulded stones he found on the Athenian Akropolis for their mathematical basis rather than for working out how they might have been achieved. He established that the shape of the rise in the Parthenon stylobate was close to a parabola and that the entasis on the pillars, the echinus moulding on the capitals, the soffit of the corona to the pediment, as well as other smaller profiles were hyperbolic.   On this basis he suggested in his letter from Athens to the Secretary of the Society of Dilettanti, dated 6th. February 1847 that the knowledge of conic sections by Greek architects preceded the investigations of that subject by the school of Plato.

This may be so, but not necessarily. Penrose had observed that the profiles of the entasis on the arrises had greater regularity of curvature than could be ascertained on the vertical surface within the flutes, particularly on those away from direct sunlight; so much depended on the skill of the masons employed and the experience of the architects directing them. In thinking that the moulding profiles were all mathematically based, perhaps Penrose underestimated the instincts of the architects of the Parthenon for the beauty of these subtle natural forms. It took only a sensitively informed freehand line to define the outline of a mason's pattern, and it is clear from the profiles of contemporary pottery and the confident line drawings on them that such sensitivity was relatively widespread.

How this was achieved by the masons is another matter. In the same letter from Athens Penrose had remarked on the peculiarity of the Parthenon pillars that the flutes are deeper in proportion to their width as they progress upward. This may be a way of expressing that their depth was relatively constant while the flutes narrowed, and he wondered how any practical pattern for the flutes themselves could have been made or used for these circumstances.

He also reported that it was in the top drum that the flute profiles below were reconciled with those already cut on the neck of the capitals, which were lifted into position before the fluting process took place, a strong indication that the cutting of the flutes started at the base. At the capital the flutes were 5mm less deep at their centre than those below, while the radius into the arris was 117mm compared with 120mm at the base of the earlier Parthenon pillars. On his plate 46 Penrose had drawn the shape of the arris on the base from the earlier Parthenon and found it to be the same as that on the later Parthenon. So perhaps the masons were equipped with a wooden pattern defining how the arris should be rather than the whole flute, as this seems to be the only constant form connected with the fluting on the pillars. This would leave the varying distance between the arrises to be developed by the individual masons into flatter curves according to their skill and their sensibility.[17]

The aesthetic purpose of the flutes was not merely to emphasise the pillar's roundness or make variable shadows on the stone. Just as a square pillar is much broader viewed on its diagonal, so a fluted pillar has two diameters which can be seen, measured by Penrose as differing by only 25mm on the Parthenon. A moving eye notices this perhaps only subconsciously as the pillar is perceived to pass from one thickness to the other and back again, suggesting it possesses a flickering animation. The fluting of the pillars was a contribution as important as their leaning, their tapering and their entasis to the enlivening of the whole temple structure. Even when the eye is still, the movement of the shadows cast by the abacus of the capital, and by the flutes themselves, measures out the ever changing time of day and season in a delightful way.

Yet the individual pillars were themselves only elements in the design of a temple which had to speak in simpler terms from a great distance. The earlier Parthenon had been designed to be raised aloft on an artificial foundation so that it could be seen from anywhere in the city and beyond as a whole, complete. By standing directly on the new raised ground level within the sanctuary, the later version became something very different, far

---

[17] It is a measure of the skills developed by the masons working on the Parthenon that by the time the flutes on the larger pillars of the Propylaia needed to be cut (there were only twelve required) there were masons capable of cutting flutes which were profiled as a single segment of a circle, in such a way that the depth of the flutes varied continuously all the way up the pillars so that the radius of the segment equalled the diminishing distance between the arrises.

from simple. It passed from being an object and became a spatial presence, a place to move around, to enter and move within. Having drawn men to it, as some vast magnet, it was fashioned to reward the eye at each stage of proximity by unfolding fresh details of carving and, closer still, even of delicately painted leaves on mouldings and, on flat fascias, geometric frets that ran like coloured stitching to define the top edge of the massive architrave beams. And throughout it all, the pillars, given a profile of such intrigue that they proposed an equally fascinating converse edge to the intervals between them, beat out a rhythm through the whole assembly, changing stride only at the ends, as a runner would to turn a corner.

(10) How the stones were moved

Manolis Korres's drawings in 'From Pentelicon to the Parthenon' show how stones could have been manhandled from the quarry to the haulage wagon, stationed at a raised loading dock. Presumably a similar unloading dock was constructed on the Akropolis for transferring stones from the wagon to sleds on which they could be moved, using rollers, to where they would be worked. Half way through the working, as has been shown, the stone had to be turned over - in the case of the lowest drum of each pillar, without damaging the few centimetres of the sharp arrises already cut there. Levering, similar to the procedure in the quarry, would turn the drum on to its curved side but using fine quarry waste as a cushion for the next and final stage of overturning would have been risky - it could conceal stones which were not so fine, stones which could damage the short lengths of the sharp arrises which had been cut on the base of the lowest pillar drums, a hazard not to be risked. Hides sewn

70

together and tightly packed with straw[18] could have been the preferred cushion, overlapping the edges of the sled timbers which would then be used to transport the stone to the hoisting location.   Any architect organising these site operations would have wished these procedures to be carried out on the highest ground of the Akropolis so that the heavy haulage wagon, already loaded in the quarry by others, would deposit the stones at a level which allowed the final delivery to the hoisting position to be either on the level or slightly downhill.   It is quite likely that, at the east end, the rise of the stylobate step and the two below would be covered temporarily with waste material to form a level approach for hand hauled transport to the actual erection site, using sleds and rollers.   Such waste was already being used to raise up the ground levels to the south of the temple.

The raising up of the stones to place them in position would have had to be done by a team of men operating a hoisting device, such as a crane.   Unfinished pillar drums with projecting ears of stone still in place, to which hoisting tackle would have been attached, were found buried in the filled ground at the time of the site excavation carried out in the 1880's (fig.12); presumably they were unsuitable for use through faults discovered in the stone or in the manner in which they had been partially worked. The unfinished walls of the Propylaia show each stone with such ears still remaining on the centre of the long face, shaped to enable the stone to be hoisted by the sling of a crane.   Where stones met at a vertical joint the adjoining ends were worked to a close fit only around the perimeter edges, the centre being slightly recessed, a feature known as the anathyrosis.   This allowed a perfect fit to be achieved by rubbing the meeting edges while the weight of the stone was still being held by the sling and the crane, the gearing of the crane allowing minute movements of

---

[18] A profitable contract for the young Kleon, whose father was a tanner?

Fig. 24 LIFTING EARS LEFT ON UNFINISHED STONES ON THE PROPYLAIA

the stone to be controlled while the adjustments to the meeting faces were being carried out.   On smaller structures dressed ashlar blocks in the walls could be levered into place.

(11)   The scaffolding plan

A clue to the dimensions of the scaffolding arrangement required for the building is the thin stone disc mounted on a timber framework, mentioned earlier.   Whether this was used to indicate high spots on the stone drums or for grinding them off, it would need to be applied to the stones in situ within the scaffolding and at ground level on the next drum waiting to be raised.   Its dimensions therefore tell us something of how the scaffolding would have had to be arranged.   The purpose of the scaffolding was to support the masons guiding their stones into final position, and afterwards while they prepared the stone to receive the next course.   The clear area around the stone had to be enough for men to work at it and pass each other while they did so and, in the case of the Parthenon, to operate the placing and possibly the rotating of the stone disc within the space defined by the scaffold poles.   The reduced pillar centres dimension at the corners suggests a suitable scaffolding module of 1.842m in plan. (see fig.25 m and n)   This would allow relatively light timbers to be used, an obvious advantage in terms of availability and ease of manhandling.   Eight round poles for each pillar, notched to receive horizontal plank supports on the inside and diagonal braces on the outside would allow sections of prefabricated scaffold frames to be lifted into position, then pegged and tied together.   The same module of 1.842m could have suited the vertical dimensions, where the working platform needed to be raised in units of about 0.9m, to allow comfortable access to all eleven stone drums.   (At certain corner locations there were only ten drums but this would not have proved to be a complication).   Connections between successive lifts of scaffold

Fig. 25 STUDY FOR THE PARTHENON CRANE

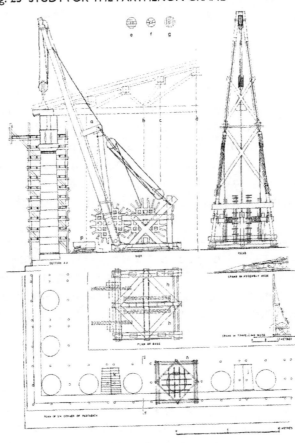

a	Broken lines indicating the position of the naos wall and its stepped base.
b	Centre line of pillars in the naos.
c	Centre line of pillars in the treasury.
d	Centre line of the temple.
e.f.g	Components of the pulley wheels.
h	Zone for counterweights.
j	Architect's working drawing on the pavement for the adjacent pillars, with horizontals drawn full size and verticals to one quarter of full size.
k	The same with the mason's record of the height of each finished stone drum laid, thereby defining the base

diameter of the next.

m The sixteen-handled framework carrying the stone disc for revealing slight irregularities, or for grinding them away, shown in position within the scaffolding.

n Plan of scaffolding framework, of 150mm diameter verticals in 1.842m lengths, inner timbers set horizontal to support the working platform decking, and outer timbers raked to stiffen the assembly.

P The next cornice stone to be lifted into place, delivered to the hoisting zone on a cushion and cradle run on rollers.

74

poles could be simply made using collar coupling units fabricated possibly with up to eight smaller diameter timbers stitched together with twine, wrapped around the meeting points of the superimposed posts, and then lashed with rope to make them secure.   Such connections would be most conveniently placed midway between the decking levels to avoid the joints of horizontal and raking framing elements with the posts.   Above the level of the pillar capitals, a continuous horizontal working platform was required, inside and out, for the assembly of the entablature.   This could have been cantilevered out on extended raking cross braces between the pillars, with intermediate raking supports stabilised against the pillars themselves.   The module of 1.842m centres of scaffold poles would have allowed the overhanging cornice stone to be within the outer support line.

(12)   Why the peristyle had to be erected first

When this arrangement is drawn it can be seen that the walls and pillars could not possibly have been built at the same time, nor could the naos with the pronaos and opisthodomos pillars have been built before the peristyle, as Penrose believed.[19]   The stone pillar drums weighed up to 9 tonnes and the counterbalancing problem of any hoisting method would require

---

[19] Penrose p.12 n.4, where he assumed that the naos, together with the pronaos and posticum pillars were built before the peristyle, an order of erection which would have been impossible on this foundation due to the lack of space at the west and south for the delivery of the stones to be hoisted and for the crane itself, the ground level being too far below the working platform at the time of the building of the earlier Parthenon, for which the same system of erection would have had to be employed..   The argument he used to explain the difference in diameter of the pronaos pillars from those outside the west end of the treasury, namely that the architects considered that those at the east end, which he assumed were built first, were too thin, necessitating an increase in diameter for those at the west end, could equally well apply to the circumstance where the west end pillars were built first and were then considered to be too fat, requiring a reduction at the east end.

them to be delivered by sled to a point as close as possible to the scaffolding surrounding the pillar for which they were intended. This delivery zone overlaps the line of the steps to the naos level so, while the peristyle was being erected, these steps could not be in position either.   The marble stylobate stones were the primary elements determining the final levels of the peristyle pavement but, apart from them, and any local extension of the surface level where the architect's pillar outline was to be drawn, it is likely that the whole of the rest of the solid foundation of stone was left unpaved, at a level slightly below that of the stylobate stones, until all the superstructure of the peristyle was erected.   Only after the later erection of the naos walls would the stone of the sub-base platform be cut away to a depth allowing the marble pavement to be placed in the peristyle area.

(13)   A possible form of the hoisting crane

With such an extensive clear working surface, the hoisting device could have taken the form drawn in figure 25.   This is based on the progressively multiple pulley systems designed to handle increasing loads which are described by Vitruvius.[20] Throughout his book he made constant references to the Greek practice from which Roman architects had learned their skills.

Painters and carvers are notoriously unreliable as sources for the ancient design of cranes.   Because of the demands of their own disciplines, they are liable to take liberties with scale, distorting it to suit the dimensional limitations of the pictorial image they are creating and, for similar reasons, simplifying or omitting altogether important details of construction and application which would be vital in any meaningful reconstruction of what the machine was actually like.   For instance, the scene of a

---

[20] Vitruvius 'The Ten Books on Architecture' Book ten 2.

76

building site shown in the painting from the 'caldarium' in the villa of San Marco, Stabiae, and the reconstruction made from it[21] shows a machine capable of only raising and lowering a stone over the same spot.   This may be of some limited use in construction work using small stones, such as on some walls where, if the load can be pulled into place over the wall line, it can then be distributed on rollers to where it is to be set.   But it would be ineffective in any larger works where, once it was raised, horizontal movement of the load in the air would also be required.   By showing the jib restraints merely anchored into the ground and immovable, this version exhibits a lack of understanding of the methods or the forces required to adjust the angle of the jib and thereby move the load horizontally, forces which can be greater than those needed to raise the load from the ground.   The stationary nature of the machine is a serious limitation of its usefulness.   The funerary relief of the family of the Haterii, shows a more powerful and complicated crane, but the vital information of what lies at the other end of the jib anchoring and adjusting ropes is missing from the scene.   The omission of this important detail does not imply that the crane was a crude device, but that the carver considered the picture's interest to lie elsewhere.

It has been shown that when a pillar drum was placed in position, some time and labour needed to be spent preparing it to receive the next one, and only when that was done could the team of masons finally determine the base diameter of the next stone to be made ready for lifting into position.   The crane and the team of operators could not be kept waiting so long when there were so many similar pillars to be assembled.   That is why the cranes used to erect any building where an extended entablature was supported by a series of pillars, would have

---

[21] figs. 88 and 89 in J-P Adam's 'Roman Building, Materials and Techniques'

been made to be mobile.   The design parameters for the Parthenon crane could be summarised as follows:

1. Maximum load to be hoisted, 18 tonnes. (2 only - lintels over doors)
2. Maximum regular load 13 tonnes. (architrave beams)
3. Maximum height of travel of load above lifting position, 19 metres.
4. Horizontal displacement of load when raised, up to 6 metres.
5. Range of working angle of jib when under load, 90 - 70 degrees.
6. Crane to be capable of being assembled on the ground and raised to its working attitude.
7. Crane to be able to be moved when assembled.

The crane design would consist of two main assemblies, the jib and the base frame, within which would be mounted the moving parts.   These assemblies would be constructed of pine with oak used for moving parts and bearings.   Iron bindings would be used where required.   Iron chain is shown used for frame members solely in tension.   Best hemp would be used for the ropes.

1   The jib has two arms, each tapering from 750 x 300mm to 450 x 250mm and 23m long, stiffened by 500 x 300mm struts housed into the jib arms and stayed by an iron chain passed through the arm and the strut via iron plates and anchored at the rear.

2   The jib arms are bound with iron at the foot, where they bear on similarly iron-lined recesses in the base frames, also beneath the pulley mounting socket, and at the top where the two arms are joined by a spacer and an iron tie   Iron binding is also used where the raking struts are housed into the arms.

3   The jib arms are joined lower down by crossed braces, 300 x 200mm, pegged and lashed to the arms, and by a 500 x 150mm

spacer, notched under the raking struts and pegged and lashed to the upright struts.

4   To facilitate assembly on the ground, the pair of winding wheels which activate the raising and lowering of the load pulleys, are shown mounted on a sub-axle, itself set in rocker arms pivoting on a combined axle/spacer between the bottom of the jib arms.

5   The other major assembly, the base frame, is shown built from 500 x 300mm timbers, the lower members set horizontally to facilitate movement on iron rollers below them.   The diagonal elements are to keep the assembly rigid and square, while also making the whole base easier to turn.   The bearing elements above are used vertically, notched over the lower members and tied to them with iron rods and wedges passed through slots in the rods.   The two outer bearers are each doubled and set at the same angle as the arms of the jib.   Sandwiched between the double members, and dovetailed into them, are set the upstanding members of the base frame, which also incline at the same angle as the jib arms.   They carry between them the horizontal axle, 400 x 400mm square and 400mm diameter at the bearings.   The axle is also supported centrally by another crossed frame, mounted vertically and similarly anchored to the base framework.   When the axle with its pair of winding wheels is in position, double horizontal members, 500 x 150mm, halved where they meet the crossed framework, are pegged and lashed to retain the axle in position.   Inset bearings of hardwood, shaped to accommodate the angles of the outer framework, provide replaceable parts for the points of wear.   A horizontal spacer, 500 x 150mm connects the two outer inclined frames near their top.

6   Floor timbers, resting on the base framework, provide a working platform for the operators and a support for the stone counterweights in areas 'h', required to prevent the crane overturning.

7   Pulley systems, reducing the loads by a theoretical factor of five, are made up of 'e', outer discs, 'f' bearing wheels, and 'g', a central disc, all constructed of 75mm oak planks riveted together with hard bronze.   These are mounted on square axles, rounded at the bearings.   All the pulley assemblies are mounted in iron bound pine sub-frames.

8   The winding wheels are similarly assembled in sandwich construction, consisting of 200 x 100mm outer framework halved together to secure 125 x 100mm intermediate radials which provide the support for steps not supplied by the outer gridwork structure. The winding wheels activating the raising and lowering of the stonework consist of 20 radials, the outer 300mm of which bear cantilevered steps (not shown) wide enough to accommodate two men 'climbing' the wheel side by side.   The axle on which the rope is wound has a diameter of 333mm and the effective radius of the wheel assembly is 1.666metres, providing a theoretical load reduction factor of 10.   These wheels are set apart 2.8 metres. The wheels activating the adjustment of the angle of the jib are larger to cope with the greater effort needed. They have an axle of 400mm diameter, 24 radials to accommodate extra manpower, and an effective radius on them of 2 metres, giving a similar load reduction factor of 10.   The jib can be locked in any position by inserting a length of stout timber through the wheel to engage with the central supporting framework of the base, freeing the operators to work on the hoisting wheels.

9   The forces involved are as follows:

9.1   Lifting the heaviest load (18 tonnes) determines the rope thickness.   The pulley ratio reduces this to 3.6te in the rope. Best hemp (utilising one sixth of its breaking stress) can support this on 50mm diameter rope.   Since only two of these loads are present, extra manpower can be called upon to raise them.

9.2   The heaviest standard load is 13 tonnes.   The pulley ratio reduces this to 2.6te, and the wheel/axle ratio makes it

0.26te, or 0.13te on each of the two wheels.   Each wheel can accommodate two men 'climbing' the wheel and their combined self weight would account for most of this, allowing for friction forces.   Two more men at ground level, one pushing and one pulling, at the opposite side of the wheel, would control the rise and fall.

9.3   With each load, the angle of the jib arm needs to be adjusted within the range 90-70 degrees and the force acting on the ropes attached to each arm is 14.7 tonnes.   The pulley systems here reduce this to 2.94te, which can be supported on a 50mm diameter rope.

9.4   The winding wheel ratio on this axle further reduces the load to 0.294te, or 0.147te on each wheel, a load within the scope of the same hoisting team.

10   The crane would have been assembled on the foundation platform.   The base would be put together first and the jib arms joined together resting on the base.   Levering the head of the jib assembly above the base floor level would enable the angle adjusting wheels to raise the jib into a vertical position where it would meet the horizontal members of the base side frames, preventing it moving further.   In this secure travelling mode the crane could then be manoeuvred to its working location.

The construction of such a crane would have been well within the scope of the technology available to 5th century BC. Athenian builders so their own design for hoisting machines, benefiting from a hundred years of experience, is likely to have been more refined than the example drawn.   This has been vetted for design efficiency by structural engineers using the latest analytical techniques.

(14) Sequence of operations in the building of the Parthenon

Figures 26 to 33 show the sequence of erection such a crane

Fig. 26 PLAN OF ERECTION STAGE ONE, WEST FRONT

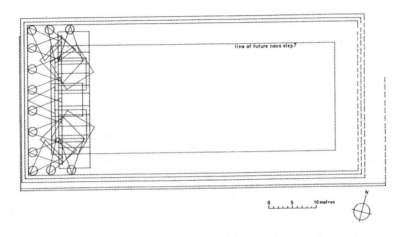

Fig. 27 STAGE TWO, NORTH AND SOUTH FLANK PILLARS, using two cranes

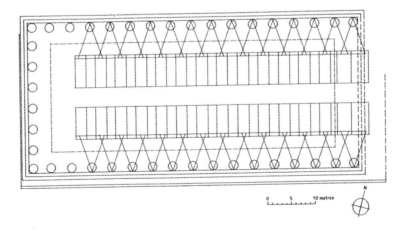

Fig. 28 STAGE THREE, OPISTHODOMOS PILLARS AND MARBLE CEILING OVER PERISTYLE

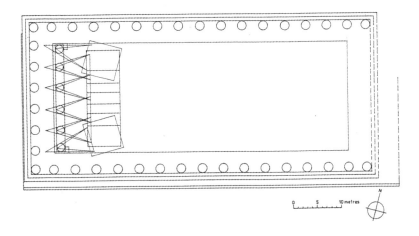

Fig. 29 STAGE FOUR, WEST WALL, MARBLE CEILING OVER LOBBY, NORTH AND SOUTH WALLS, CEILING OVER FLANK PERISTYLES, using two cranes

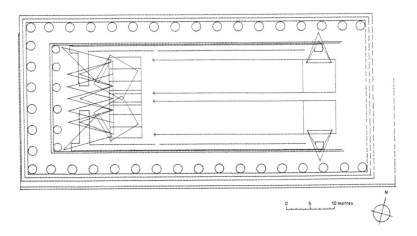

Fig. 30 STAGE FIVE, TREASURY PILLARS AND CEILING BEAMS, using two cranes

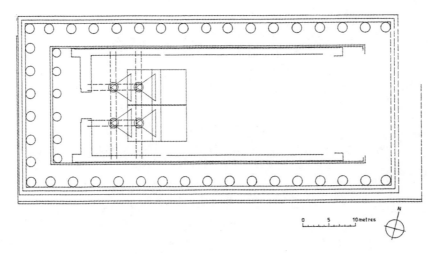

Fig. 31 STAGE SIX, WALL BETWEEN NAOS AND TREASURY, BEAMS OVER TREASURY AND PILLARS IN NAOS WITH CEILING BEAMS, one crane only

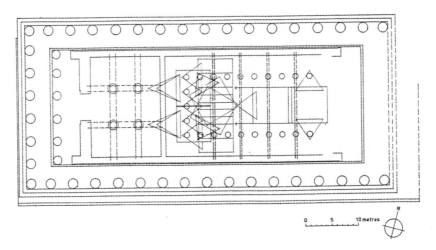

Fig. 32 STAGE SEVEN, EAST WALL, PRONAOS PILLARS AND MARBLE CEILING OVER

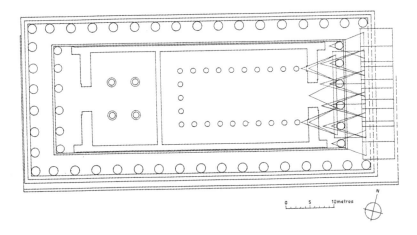

Fig. 33 STAGE EIGHT, EAST FRONT AND CEILING OVER

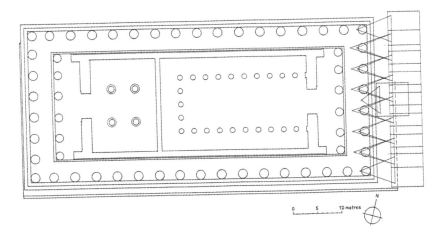

could manage, operating on the platform foundation within the peristyle. Two cranes could work together until the interior pillars in the naos had to be set up. Only at the east end would the hoisting need to be effected outside the temple structure. The stone coffered ceiling panels over the peristyle would be lifted into position once the walls were raised to that level, allowing finishing to proceed below and roof construction to be started above, working from west to east. This system of assembly would allow all trades to join in the building activity at the earliest possible date, ensuring a speedy completion, and it can be shown that the building period recorded in the Parthenon Building Accounts is realistic. The figure of Athene, designed by Pheidias, was covered with panels of ivory and gold. It would have been made on a timber framework, all of which, because of its size, would have been pre-fabricated and erected piece by piece in a workshop before being taken down, its parts moved into the temple and then re-assembled as soon as the temple construction was ready to receive it. The final assembly of the framework for the statue of Athene would have been possible when the placing of the marble roof tiles was still only half complete and before the naos doors were hung. From his reading of the Building Accounts, Dinsmoor understood the latter event to be carried out in year VIII, 440 - 439 BC.[22]

(15) The similarity of structure between the Parthenon and its predecessor

Those pieces of marble stylobate stones and pillar drums which have survived from the earlier Parthenon were similar in size to the stones used on the later Parthenon, so the problems of handling and hoisting them into place would have been identical, and the methods employed would also have been the same,

---

[22] A.J.A. vol.XXV 1921 p.243.

except that, the naos being narrower, only one crane could have been used.   This is known because the excavation of 1885-90 revealed that the podium foundation supporting the Parthenon had been widened along the north flank to accommodate a wider temple, one with eight pillars at the east and west ends.   The original foundation, designed in the early 480's, must have been intended for a temple with six pillars at each end.

(16)   The significance of the naos step stones of the Parthenon

B.H.Hill drew attention in 1912 to a feature of the Parthenon whose significance was not recognised at the time.   He wrote,

"The lower step of the cella of the present Parthenon is composed in large part of re-used blocks from the earlier temple.   This is shown, in the case of all of them that can be examined, by the fact that they have two sets of clamp cuttings.   Those of the first set, from which the clamps have been removed by orderly chiselling, do not match in the adjacent stones; those of the second set always do so match, and the clamps, when they are missing, have been hacked out in the manner usual to modern searchers for lead.   Clearly only these latter clamps belong to the existing temple.   Now the blocks thus proved to have been put to an earlier use are on the average 1.77m long.   This is a standard length (six Solonian feet) in the sub-structure of the older Parthenon, but it is not normal for the present Parthenon.   It is, however, the average length of twenty of the twenty-nine blocks of the lower step of the north side of the cella and of a number on the other sides.   All of these had doubtless been used on the older Parthenon."

(Hill referred to the earlier Parthenon as the 'Older' Parthenon) As long as scholars consider, on the basis of surmise alone, without demonstrable proof, that it was possible to build a temple as large as the Parthenon by erecting walls at the same time as pillars, or the naos before the peristyle on this particular site, these step stones below the naos hold little significance. Smaller temples, such as the Hephaisteion and the Temple of Aphaia on Aigina, which have dimensions roughly half those of the Parthenon, posed the challenge of weights of comparable parts which were less than one quarter of those of the larger temple, (for instance, pillar drums weighing 1.6 tonnes, compared with 7 tonnes). Consequently they would require hoisting tackle of relatively modest dimensions, allowing perhaps a different process and technique of erection to be considered. Figure 66 shows the peristyle of the Temple of Aphaia drawn to the same scale alongside the earlier Parthenon to illustrate the point. With building components on the scale of those used on both the Parthenon and its predecessor, it would have been impossible to build the walls until the peristyle with its entablature was completed, as this study has demonstrated. So the presence of stones which had been placed in position to form the naos step of an earlier temple is also evidence that the perimeter pillars of that earlier temple had been erected complete to cornice level.

(17)   Conclusion

Which temple was this? There are two possibilities. Either the temple started in the 480's - what may be called the pre-Persian-visit Parthenon, started before the Persian army's occupation of Athens - was much further advanced in its construction than has been generally understood, or there was a post-Persian, pre-Perikleian earlier Parthenon being built to the same or similar design as the 480's BC. original.

There are two major objections to the first of these possibilities. The first is this. There would not have been enough time to erect both the foundation platform and a substantial part of the temple in the eight years available.   Even allowing for the foundation platform of the dismantled Hekatompedon remaining as part of the present foundation, over 11,000m^3 of stone and marble would have had to be brought to the site to achieve the stylobate level of the earlier Parthenon.   Considering that the total volume of finished stonework in the Perikleian Parthenon was about 9,400m^3, and that there was 2,600m^3 in the Propylaia, a completely new building which took five years to build, it can be seen that transporting and placing the stone for the temple foundation - even though this was a simple exercise - and the marble for the stylobate of the earlier Parthenon, would have left little time for erecting many parts of that temple's superstructure.

The second objection is this.   The only parts of this earlier temple's superstructure which have remained in a fire-damaged state after the Persian destruction are fourteen bottom drums, presumably six from the west end and four from each of the north and south flanks adjoining, together with a number of additional drums to be placed above them.   It seems that the crew of the single crane used to erect this first part of the structure in the 480's was expected to keep pace with fourteen teams of masons preparing stones for hoisting.   This is very similar to the ratio suggested in figures 26 to 33 for the erection pattern of the later Parthenon.   Five opisthodomos porch pillar bases from the earlier Parthenon were also discovered; possibly one of them had been flawed, as only four would have been required for stage three of the assembly process to build the earlier Parthenon.   This surviving evidence points to a post-Persian earlier Parthenon being the original home for the re-used naos steps. The following study will show that many more parts of the Parthenon measured by Penrose exhibit signs that they have been re-cycled from previous use on this post-Persian earlier temple.

Fig. 34 SETTING OUT PLAN OF EARLIER PARTHENON WITH WORK STARTED AT THE WEST
END

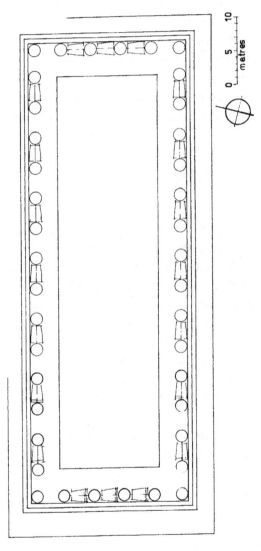

**STUDY 3   PRECISION, SUBTLETY AND ABERRATION IN
THE DESIGN OF THE PARTHENON**

Study 2 has shown that the dimensioned drawings published by
Penrose in 1851 give an unexpected insight into how the temple
would have been built.   They also reveal anomalies of detail in
the assembly of the inner parts of the peristyle which have been
disregarded hitherto, or dismissed as "accidental variations or
workmen's errors".[1]   There was nothing erroneous about some of
them; they were very expensive, carefully considered and often
ingenious measures devised by the architects of the later
Parthenon in their endeavours to re-use the larger elements of
marble work necessarily taken from the earlier temple, in ways
which would have no detrimental effect on what was to be seen.
Indeed, what was produced by the designers was recognised in
its own time, and has been so ever since, as exceeding the
quality of every other work of architecture built in an era which
was characterised by brilliance.   The amount of extra labour
which had to be committed to this task of amendment was great
and it is a mark of the skill with which it was devised and carried
out that none of it was perceptible to the human eye while the
temple was intact.   Equally, no-one since his day has recognised
the significance of what Penrose saw and recorded of these
obscure parts of the Parthenon.

Until Penrose recorded precise measurements of all the
deviations from the vertical, the horizontal and the straight
which exist on the Parthenon, no-one had known what they were
in dimensional terms. His drawings confirmed that the suspected
entasis and taper on the pillars was real, and moreover, that
they leaned inwards; that the pavement supporting the pillars
did rise towards the centre of each façade in a gentle curve.   The

---

[1] Dinsmoor 'Architecture of Ancient Greece' 1950 p.164n2

Fig. 35 PENROSE'S PLATE 7

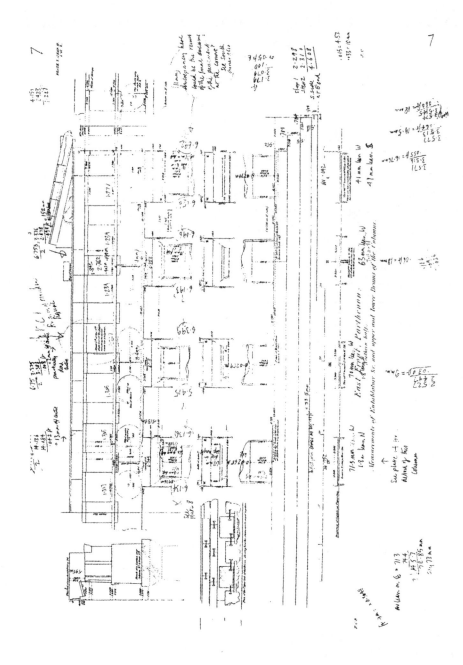

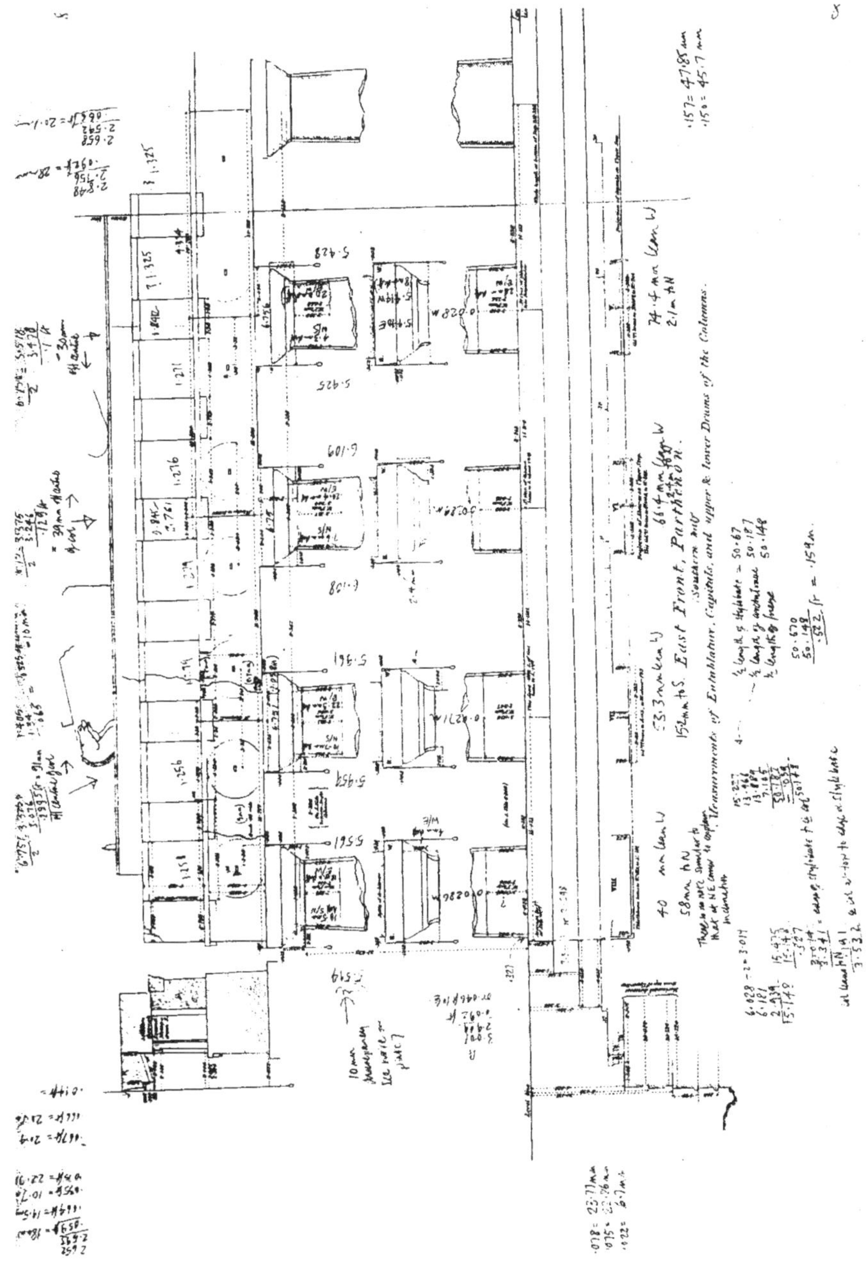

Fig. 36 PENROSE'S PLATE 8

verification itself was probably enough for most people interested in the subject, apart from the few like W.B. Dinsmoor who expressed the dimensions and deviations in terms which British and American scholars at the time could appreciate, feet, inches and fractions of inches.[2]   Since then the metric system of measurement has been increasingly accepted as a standard, and Dinsmoor's description of these subtleties in 1950 is rapidly becoming as obscure as Penrose's decimalisation of the foot, so the following pages may be helpful in bringing to a wider readership the degree of subtlety aimed at, and achieved, by the Athenian architects of the 5th century BC.

(1)   The inclination of the pillars.

Penrose measured the amount of inclination on the pillars of the east front by dropping plumb lines from adjacent faces of the abacus, and recorded it on plates 7and 8 (see figs. 35 and 36) He described in the text the difficulty he encountered with the method, owing to the frequent breeze which blew on the Akropolis, making it rarely possible to rely on it over the great height of the pillars - about 10.44 metres.   The measurements appear to show a variation of lean towards the west from 40mm and 41mm at the corners, to 71.3mm and 74.4mm near the centre.   He explained this difference as being a distortion due to the effect of the explosion which took place in 1687 while gunpowder was being stored in the temple by the Turks. However, on the same plates, Penrose recorded the lengths of the stones forming the architrave beam course,   noting the widths of

---

[2] A.A.G. p.149 - 173, complicated by his use also of what he called the Doric foot. On p.165 he expressed the lean on the pillars as two and three/eighth inches, which is 60mm.   This is not a translation of any dimension given by Penrose for this feature of the design. It was most likely to be either a translation of a metric dimension from N. Balanos, or a measurement taken by himself. If it was measured after the intervention of Balanos's work on the Parthenon, it cannot be taken as deriving from the original structure.

Fig. 37 PENROSE'S PLATE 16

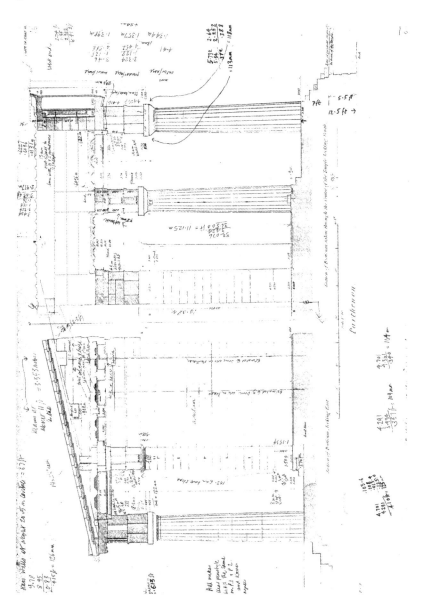

a number of cracks and joints which had opened due to earthquake and explosive shocks, which totalled 43.4mm. When allowance is made for these accidental effects, the final overall dimension can be compared with the centre to centre dimension between the two corner pillars at their base to establish that the inward lean of each pillar along the flanks of the temple was originally 79mm.

There is insufficient information about the levels of the pavement at the rear of each pillar on the fronts to allow the calculation of lean to be made based on the slope formed on the top of the lowest drums, the method used by the builders to achieve it. The nearest pavement record along the E/W centre line of the temple would suggest that, using the builders' method, the inclination at the west may have been 59mm and, at the east, 89mm.   The pavement levels at the west were distorted by a thousand years of wear after the conversion of the temple into a church.   The approach during that time was from the west, with steps formed to a human scale cut into the higher temple steps. Across the peristyle pavement at the east the rise of slope measured by Penrose was 21mm, but at the west only 8mm, some of the difference probably caused by wear.   During classical times the number of visitors actually entering the temple must have been comparatively few.   Making an allowance at the west for this wear, the inclination of the pillars, assessed by this method, may have been between 70 and 80mm.

(2)   Inclinations of other structural elements.

Penrose's plate 16 (see fig.37) also shows how the end face of the anta walls leaned towards the top of the opisthodomos pillars 114mm. Why this was done is obscure. In the plane of the two anta faces their inclination would have been seen against the central flute of the peristyle pillars beyond, which was vertical.

The amount of inclination given to the face of the anta was much less than the inclined edge of the pillar resulting from its tapering, so there was no correspondence there either.   The outward lean of the anta face was equal in amount to the inward inclination of the outer face of the naos wall around the corner, so that in the three-quarter view the two slopes would have cancelled each other out. Perhaps that was the intention.   Had the anta face leaned the other way, back instead of forward, a sensible and comprehensible relationship would have been set up with all the neighbouring pillars.   It seems to have been either an unclear instruction wrongly carried out and never corrected, or a playful device based on caprice and, as such, lacking the integrity and poetry of the other deliberate deviations from the plumb.

The vertical faces of each abacus were given an inclination to make them appear to be at right angles to the not quite horizontal lines of the architrave beams above, both in elevation and section. See figs. 35 and 36.

(3)   The upward curve of the stylobate.

The reasons which have been suggested for shaping the surface on which the pillars stood into a curve, range from the poetic - that it responded to a line beloved of most Greeks, the sea's horizon - to the prosaic - that it was needed to shed rainwater from the pavement.   Penrose's measurements show that there were also two tectonic purposes, one purely aesthetical, the other practical.

When he measured the remains of the Parthenon in 1846-7 the surface and some upper courses of the podium foundation on which it stood had been uncovered. This revealed two surprising

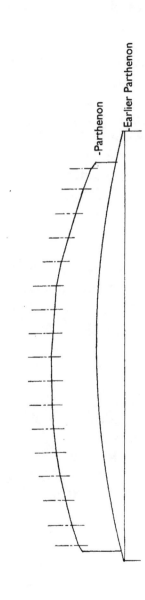

Fig. 38 STYLOBATE CURVE ON PARTHENON AND EARLIER PARTHENON COMPARED

features which had not been seen since about 430 BC when the foundation had been buried by the final raising of the terrace to the west and south of the temple to the level of the base of the three steps making up the krepidoma.   The first was that the original foundation platform had been extended towards the north.   This was to accommodate the Perikleian Parthenon, designed with eight pillars across its front, so it was obvious that the original foundation had been constructed for a temple intended to be six pillars wide.

The stylobate of the earlier Parthenon was the only part of that temple to be completely assembled by 480 BC.   We know this because fire damage to stone pillar drums and steps belonging to that temple, damage caused by burning scaffolding, testifies that work had started on some of the pillars, and of course the stylobate had to be completed before the precise locations of all the pillars could be set out.

Penrose's plates 11 and 12 record his measurements of the rate of upward curve on the surface of the original foundation structure.   This differed between the front - 0.145/100 - and the flank - 0.105/100 - a rate of rise similar to that which he had noted in his measurement of the curvature on the stylobate of the Hephaisteion – 0.140/100 on the front and 0.097/100 on the flank. On the Parthenon stylobate he recorded rises of 0.225/100 on the front and 0.156/100 on the flank, approximately 1½ times the rate of rise on the sub-basement.

The original foundation had adopted, for its upper level, the surface of the underlying rock at the north-east corner, which was on the ridge line of the Akropolis, sloping down from east to west from that point.   At the north-west corner, Penrose noted that the rock was some 2 metres below the top. The enlargement of the original foundation northward had to be built up from this rock progressively more towards the west end to support the extended stylobate. It has been pointed out in Study 2 that all the erection activity, particularly on the earlier Parthenon, including the delivery and hoisting of the parts, must have taken place upon the foundation platform itself. No reliance could be placed upon the use of ground beyond its southern and western edges, where the ground level was being raised with fill material, which is notoriously unreliable for carrying loads in the earliest years after being placed.

The detail of the levels is summarised on figure 9. This shows that while the south-west and south-east corners of the foundation platform, built in the 480's, were set within an astonishing 2mm of level with each other, and with a rise in the centre of the south flank of 83mm, the new Parthenon stylobate was higher at the west end than at the east, but with the north-east and south-east corners again within 2mm of level with each other. The same standards of accuracy were being maintained where it mattered, but there was introduced into the 448 BC design a shrewd knowledge of what was perceptible and what was not. The degree of accuracy sought and achieved in the building of the Parthenon is impressive. Starting from a foundation platform which had been made slightly domed towards the centre, but with a degree of rise in the curvature in the longer dimension only two thirds that across the shorter, a new and larger krepidoma of three steps was erected, eccentric from the domed foundation on which it stood, and built to a more pronounced amount of curvature, giving a rise at the centre of each side 1½ times that of the original. And this was carried out in a way ensuring that the overall dimensions of the top step along the north and south edges were within 4mm of each other in a length of over 69.5 metres. It may be thought that widening the temple could have been brought about by simply extending the curve of the original stylobate to the north. But this would have resulted in the northern corners being 30mm below those of the south.   While there is a discrepancy of level on the Parthenon stylobate of 37mm between the north-west and the north-east corners, and 49mm between the south-west and the south-east, this would have been acceptable along the flanks where the general ground level was falling away in the opposite direction and over a longer distance, making the unequal levels imperceptible.   Such a difference would not have been tolerated on the horizontal lines of the main facades of the temple, nor through the rest of the structure, tilting all the roof beams out of level and the inner faces of the naos walls out of plumb.   If the entire stylobate had to be created anew it was not such an onerous extra task to reset the lines of curvature; it was done by cutting down into the top course of the foundation platform to the required depths under the steps, as shown in figure 38.

The slight curvature imparted to the earlier base structure and carried through the entire floor of the temple must have been both intended and enough to facilitate the placing and the removal of the rollers used beneath the base of the crane to allow it to be moved readily, otherwise the floor inside the naos walls would have been made flat in the north/south direction.   Why then was the curvature increased for the Perikleian Parthenon started in 448 BC if it was not necessary for constructional purposes?   If it was done to improve the appearance by increasing the 'spring' in the steps, was this an instinctive hunch on the part of the new architects?   Or, more likely, was it a judgement based on having seen the outcome resulting from the shallower curvature of an earlier design?   This would imply that the resumed building of the earlier Parthenon had reached the stage of its construction when such judgements could be reliably made.

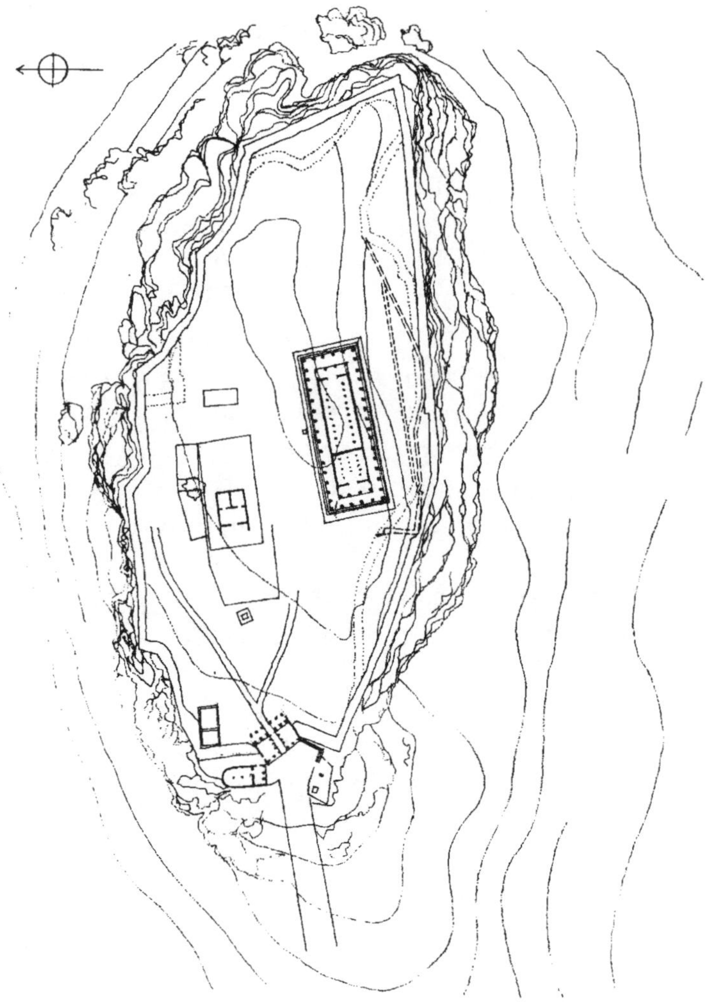

Fig. 39 PLAN OF THE ATHENIAN AKROPOLIS IN 449BC. Former line of ancient wall shown dotted, temporary retaining walls shown by broken line.

Penrose also found that the Parthenon was placed asymmetrically on the existing foundation, being located at the extreme west end of it.   Why should that have been done?   Every cubit of land to the east of the temple must have been regarded as very valuable.   Figure 39 illustrates by how much the area of the Akropolis was extended by the expensive south wall built in the time of Kimon.   In the first instance the extra space was needed during the building process to provide working room, but more importantly, to enlarge the ground area in front of the main approach to the temple.   It was to the east and north of the Parthenon that the main altar was traditionally sited, where the worshippers would gather to take part in and witness the ceremonial rites.   This would have been the main consideration in siting the Parthenon at the extreme west end of the foundation.

(4)   The regularity and the irregularity of abacus sizes.

Fig.40 shows the arrangement of abacus sizes on the Parthenon. They were recorded by Penrose on his plate 5 (fig.41) and have been translated into metric dimensions.   What is striking about them is their amazing consistency of dimension, within the west, south and east facades particularly but also, on the north flank, of nine of the thirteen remaining either in situ or fallen nearby in 1846, although there are differences between the facades. Following the precedent of the Temple of Aphaia on Aigina, the corner pillars were made larger than the others at the base and at the neck in any facade and the abacus, correspondingly, was larger.   The unusually wide abacus at the eastern corners required also a slightly less steep slope on the echinus moulding below, illustrated on Penrose's plate 19 fig. 1. (See fig.42) Penrose was convinced that the accuracy of abacus dimensions on any range, and particularly the regularity of the echinus moulding, pointed to these stones having been turned on a lathe

Fig. 40 ARRANGEMENT OF ABACUS SIZES ON THE PARTHENON

```
                                        west
        2.048   2.005   2.005   2.002    2.002   2.005   2.006   2.059

        2.003                   2.006                            2.028

        2.000           on  adjacent  face                       2.016

        2.002                                                    2.017

        2.004                                                    2.015

                much  broken                                     2.014

        2.002   fallen                                           2.014

                missing                                          2.015

south           missing           may  be  in  B.M.     2.015          north

                missing                           fallen    2.021

                missing                           fallen    2.017

        2.004   fallen                          missing

        2.002                                   fallen    2.056

        2.004                                   missing

        1.997                                            2.044

        2.002                                            2.042

        2.089   2.058   2.057   2.059    2.057   2.057   2.058   2.091

                                        east
```

Fig. 41 PENROSE'S PLATE 5

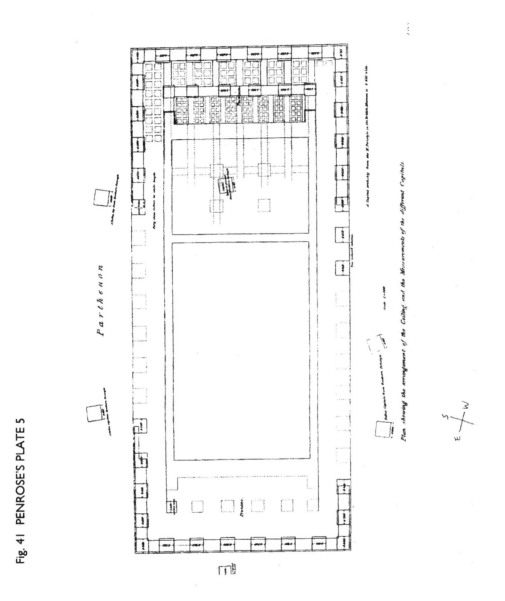

- there was 6th century precedent for this - but not everyone accepts that it was the case on the Parthenon.

What was the reason for the change in size from the west to the east front? Penrose had supposed that the erection work had commenced with the east end of the naos. Study 2 has explained how it would have been impossible to erect the peristyle with the naos in position on this site, even if it had been a procedure applicable elsewhere. The lack of manoeuvring space for the crane at the west end, and the lower ground level outside the foundation there, dictated that the west end had to be built first from the inside of the future temple, where there was a firm level foundation for the crane and the delivery points for the stones which were to be hoisted. The slight changes to the spread of the abacus at the east end must have been made by the architect after seeing the finished effect at the west end, in order to create a more solid looking support for the architrave beams, and the sculptured figures to be added to the pediments.

(5)   The layout of roof and ceiling beams and panels.

Penrose's plate 15 (see fig.43) described the layout of the ceiling beams and panels which had survived over the west end of the Parthenon. The presence on the same drawing of the pillar capitals and the ceiling beams draws attention to what appears to be a curious relationship between them. This could have been noticed by a visitor looking up, for although the ceiling beams were 2.4 metres above the pillars, they would have been seen to be out of line with them.

The odd spacing of these front peristyle beams was only possible because of the presence of a continuous carved frieze around the top of the naos and the inner porches at each end. This frieze was carved into a course of substantial marble blocks about

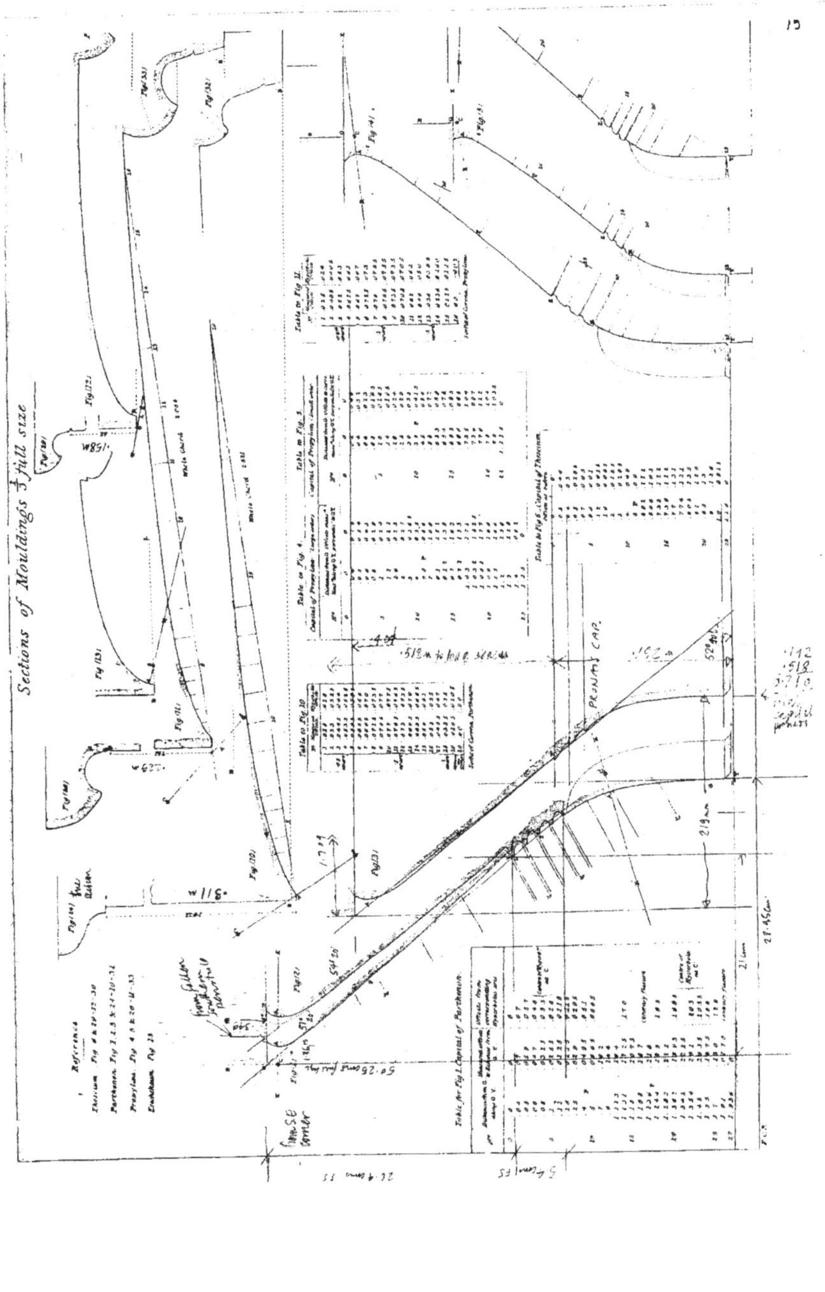

Fig. 42 PENROSE'S PLATE 19

107

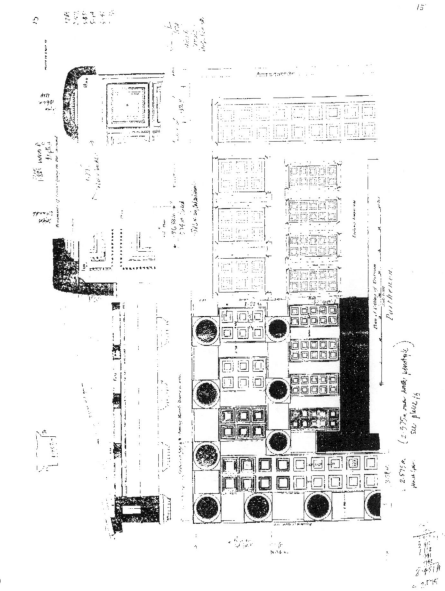

Fig. 43 PENROSE'S PLATE 15

600mm thick, capable of supporting beams placed anywhere above and spreading the load of the ceiling down through the 1.357m high composite frieze course and the 1.044m high architrave beams below it on to the pillars beneath.   The architrave beams were prepared as if a normal Doric frieze was intended above them.   Below the continuous taenia, which crowned the beams, were cut regulae and guttae centrally over the pillars and the spaces between.   Regulae were usually cut, as their name suggests, to be markers to locate the triglyphs which would be placed above.   Had such a Doric frieze been erected here, the beams across the west peristyle would have had to be aligned with the centres of the triglyphs in order to transmit their load to the architrave beams below.   Any off-beat spacing of ceiling beams over the front peristyle would have appeared to impose unsupportable loads on thin metope panels fixed between the more solid triglyphs.   So the pattern of the ceiling bays here derived from the decision to have an Ionic carved frieze over the naos.   Why, then, were the regulae and guttae, features of a Doric frieze, cut into the architrave beams?   Where a similar situation arose on the Hephaisteion a continuous moulding beneath the taenia was cut in their place, revealing an awareness on the part of its architect of the nicety of the situation.   This alertness and sensitivity is not demonstrated on the Parthenon.

Penrose had found only three beams in situ across the west peristyle in an arrangement which inferred where the others had been.   He remarked on the ceiling beams being placed in line, not with the pillar spacing below but with the roof beams above, with which they had neither visual nor structural connection, so the arrangement of beams at ceiling level was evidently merely one of dimensional convenience.   There is missing, from these and other passages of the Parthenon design, that quality of surprising inevitability which is the hallmark of the rest.

Fig. 44 DESIGN OF THE COFFERED CEILING PANELS OVER THE FLANK PERISTYLES

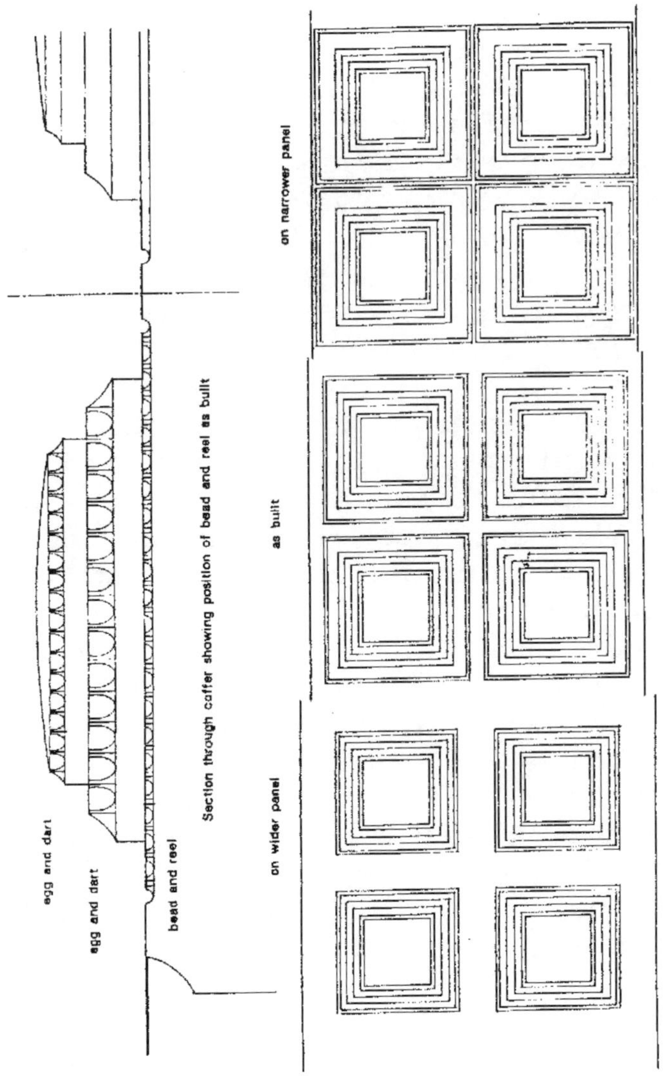

egg and dart

egg and dart

bead and reel

Section through coffer showing position of bead and reel as built

as built

on narrower panel

on wider panel

(6)   The design of the ceiling panels.

Penrose acknowledged that his indication of the coffering in the panels over the west peristyle was speculative, since at the time no fragments of them had been found.   From the overall dimensions between the beams he estimated the coffers to be not quite square, with a setting out module in the N/S direction of 1.127m and, in the E/W direction, 1.067m, compared with the square coffering over the flank peristyles, where it is 1.234m. The ceiling over the lobby outside the treasury, shown on his plate 15 (see fig. 43) was a reconstruction based on fragments of a coffer and marks within the cornice course indicating where the beams had sat.   The beams did not align in plan with those over the west peristyle.   The design of the coffer profile here is a copy of that used over the flank peristyles scaled down in the ratio 11/6.

The design of the ceiling panel coffering over the flank peristyles was both ingenious and practical.   The architects and craftsmen building a temple as large as the Parthenon could not have known precisely what size the clear ceiling width would turn out to be.   The pillars with their entablatures and the walls opposite were both made to lean through a height of over 13 metres, so the distance between them at the top could not be foreseen with absolute precision.   Figure 44 shows how the original design for the panels allowed for some variation within a range of 0.25m from the intended clear width of visible panel area.   This was done by means of a two-stage production technique.   At the first stage the coffers were set out and cut to their final detailed design, including two rows of egg and dart decoration cut into the ovolo mouldings separating the angular coffers.   All this intricacy was safely protected, being recessed into the depth of the marble panel, thereby reducing its weight.   But there was another, exposed line of bead and reel ornament which would be

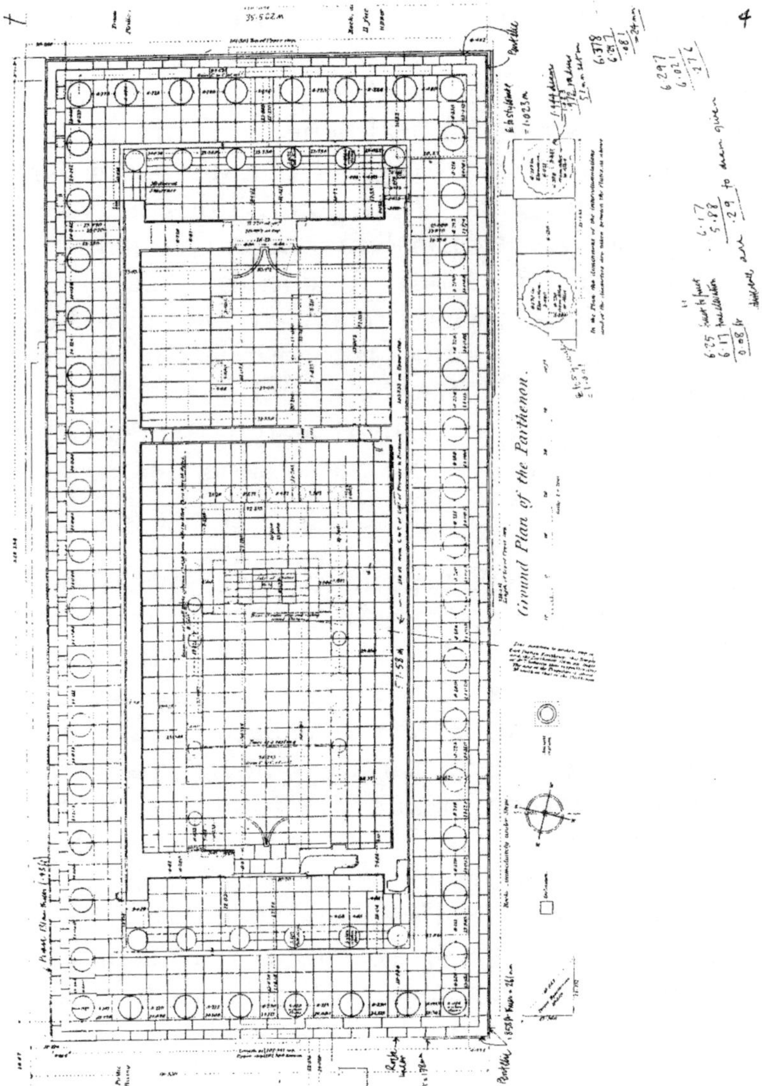

Fig. 45 PENROSE'S PLATE 4

cut last of all because it was left to stand proud of the support plane of the panel, a constant distance outside the coffers. The distance of it from the coffers could be chosen so that the space between adjacent lines of bead and reel detail was equal to the space between the bead and reel and the outer edge of the exposed panel. The dimension of the spacing which ensured this equality did not need to be predetermined. It could be defined to suit the overall width of the exposed peristyle ceiling in the N/S direction when this became known, that is, when the naos wall had reached its full height. The possible extremes are shown in figure 44. In the long E/W direction there were sufficient panel units required to make up the overall length to allow minute adjustments to be made at each joint to give the appearance of uniformity along the flank ceiling.

(7)   The layout of the roof over the treasury and the naos.

The pattern of paving stones in the treasury floor shows that four pillars had supported the roof over this area. They were so spaced (see figure 37) as to relate to recesses at roof level in the west wall, purlin locations which happen to be vertically above the ceiling beams over the peristyle across the west front, while bearing no structural relationship to them. If these purlin lines extended eastward along the whole line of roof, then they would not have been supported directly by any of the pillars erected inside the naos. A framed roof of raking timbers would have been required over this area, as shown on fig.25.

(8)   The misalignment of the heights of the peristyle and the naos walls.

The most unusual and surprising feature of the construction of the Parthenon revealed by Penrose's plate 16 (see fig.37) was the misalignment of the height of the naos walls with that of the

Fig. 46 CHANGES MADE TO ACCOMMODATE PHEIDIAS'S FRIEZE. Sections through the West peristyle on the E/W centre line.

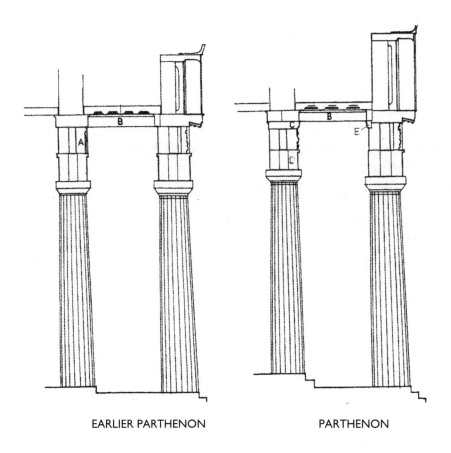

EARLIER PARTHENON   PARTHENON

peristyle structure, when each had to share the load of the marble beams and ceiling panels spanning between them.   It has been shown that the naos walls could only be built after the peristyle, including its cornice course, had been erected, so it would be expected that this later phase of construction, the naos walls, would be made to the precise height required to align with the finished peristyle.   But this was not done.   On the naos end of the connecting beams, the cornice course elements supporting the roof beams are seen to run through the width of the wall; not so at the peristyle ends, yet these were built first.   The major internal elements of the peristyle frieze were found to have been cut into, and pieces, smaller in both cross section and length, (stones E on fig.46) inserted to correct the misalignment and support the beams spanning between them.   This can only have been necessary as a result of a miscalculation.   Notes 2.13 and 2.14 give examples of how Athenian builders of the 5th century were averse to expending energy unnecessarily.   The correction of this mistake by introducing an otherwise superfluous copy of the capping course used above the carved frieze on the opposite side of the peristyle ceiling, and having to cut away the top corner section of the inner peristyle frieze to accommodate it around the whole of the perimeter of the temple, may have been an ingenious solution to an embarrassing problem but it could never be explained away as part of the intended design.   The discrepancy of heights would have been apparent first of all at the west end, during the building of stage three of the erection process - the assembly of the opisthodomos lobby pillars needed to support the earliest peristyle ceiling beams and panels - and it is here that any explanation of these curious circumstances was most likely to come to light.   The anomaly appears to be entirely out of character with the supremely competent and confident nature exhibited in carrying out the work on the peristyle.   How had this come about on an otherwise perfect work of art?

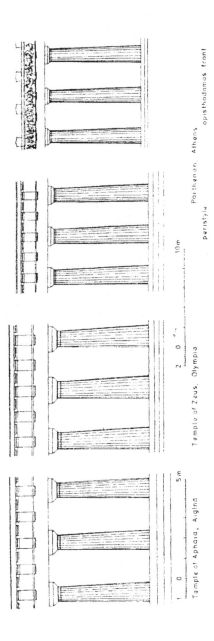

Fig. 47 ENTABLATURE PROPORTIONS COMPARED

Temple of Aphaia, Aigina

Temple of Zeus, Olympia

Parthenon, Athens

peristyle

opisthodomos front

The introduction of a string course above the carved frieze was necessary for three reasons.   (a) It would have been entirely impractical to assemble the frieze stones if they had been already carved.   Quite apart from the risk of damage to the stone edges during both the carving and the subsequent handling to place the stones in position, the final adjustment of the anathyrosis, which was worked at the ends of each stone to facilitate a perfect fit with its neighbour, was a process carried out on the stone at the time it was placed in position and, in the case of the frieze, this would have risked distorting any carving already there, where limbs and drapery crossed the joints, which they frequently did.   So the string course had to be introduced to enable the carving to take place on the stones in situ where they passed under the 1metre wide beams across the east and west peristyles.   It ensured the provision of the necessary headroom for the sculptors.   (b) The flat surface of the string course also provided a continuous visual cap to the intricate carving below, and prevented the beams across the front peristyles from appearing to sit directly on the heads of the carved figures.   (c) It also allowed roof building work to proceed above the ceiling panels while the carving of the frieze was in progress, thereby bringing more trades into action at the earliest possible time to ensure a speedy completion of the whole work.

(9)   The unusually shallow architrave beam over the opisthodomos pillars at the west.

Attention has been drawn above to the perverse cutting of Doric detail on the architrave beams over the western porch pillars when, by the time this work came to be done, an Ionic frieze was already intended; the stones for the frieze would have needed to be ordered from the quarry and cut to size while the porch pillars were being erected. The strangest feature of the architrave beams, revealed by Penrose's plate 16, (see fig.37) was their

117

unusually small height.   They measure only 1.044m compared with the sum of elements making up the frieze course above, 1.357m including the 0.344m high string course decorated with a shallow cut and coloured repeating fret pattern over the carved area.   This composite frieze is 13mm higher than the external frieze to the Parthenon.

Perhaps it was the necessity to subdivide the naos frieze course which prompted the architects to make the architrave beams below (D on fig.46) so small; they were made almost equal in height to the carved part of the frieze.   It was part of the Doric tradition that frieze and architrave were designed to be approximately equal in height.   Figure 47, which is based on J.J. Coulton's presentation to the Basel congress in 1980, illustrates how this adjustment of the inner architrave height compares with the external peristyles of the Parthenon, the Temple of Zeus at Olympia and the Temple of Aphaia on Aigina, the latter drawn to twice the scale of the others.   It left the opisthodomos architraves an unusual height in relation to the height of the pillars supporting them.   These pillars were made thinner at the base, 1.717m at the west and 1.646m at the east, than those at the perimeter which were 1.905m, reductions of about 10% and 15% respectively, while the difference between their heights was only 3.6%, 10.08m compared with 10.439m. Supported by these pillars, the architrave beams were made 29% less in height, 1.044m over the naos pillars and 1.349m high over the peristyle, the difference, 305mm, being very close to the height of the lower of the two steps on which the naos stood. Penrose measured this step on the centre line of the temple as 314mm on the north and 309mm on the south side.   Even with these opportunities to control the total height of the naos wall - the determination of the height of the two steps below the naos wall and the adjustment of the height of the architrave beam course, the naos wall still finished higher than the peristyle with its entablature, which was already in place, an illuminating reflection on the architects in charge of the Perikleian Parthenon.

(10)   The sloping external faces of the peristyle architrave beams.

Penrose's plates 7 and 8 (see figs.35 and 36) show how, by measuring offsets against a plumb line from the cornice at two places at the east end (where the stone was less severely weathered than at the west) he was able to establish that the external faces of the main peristyle architrave beams sloped inwards towards the top 16mm on their height.   The frieze elements of triglyph and metope were also inclined the same way by about the same amount.   This slight inward slope on the entablature is proportionately greater than the inclination of the axis of the pillars in the ratio 10:6.   The eye does not read the axis of the pillar but reads its profile which, on the outer edge has the line of taper added to the inclination, creating a battered effect.   Compared with the inclined profile of the pillar, that of the entablature face above looks almost plumb, a subtle combination which gives the pillars an appearance of great stability.

On plate 16, (see fig.37) similar information is recorded about the entablature over the pillars outside the treasury, but here both the architrave face and the frieze blocks above were shown to be plumb.   Around the corner, opposite the north peristyle pillars, the face of this same architrave course had been given a backward slope towards the top of just under 13mm, maintaining the line of batter given to the outer face of the naos wall.   The wall face was set back 8mm from the face of the lowest, orthostate course, which had also been given a similar backward inclination.

Fig. 48 INNER FACE OF PERISTYLE ENTABLATURE OF HEPHAISTEION

(11)   The profile of the inner face of the peristyle entablature.

The usual arrangement of stones making up the inside faces of the architrave and frieze courses of a Doric temple entablature was to make both of them plain and, most often, plumb one above the other, separated visually by a continuous plain taenia projection at the top of the architrave.   This can be seen at the Temple of Aphaia on Aigina, which predated the Parthenon, and on the Hephaisteion, fig.48, which, like the Parthenon, was built around the mid-5th century.   So it is surprising to find that Penrose had recorded detail of the arrangement on the Parthenon which was significantly different from this.   On the inside face of the peristyle entablature the architrave beam had been given an inward slope towards the top of 18.3mm, slightly greater than that formed on the outer face where it was intended for conscious aesthetical effect.   No-one could have perceived the batter given to the inner face.   Instead of the projecting taenia band which would normally have crowned the inner architrave, there was no projection at all but a 36.5mm set back to the frieze course, and this in turn was battered a further 24mm towards the cornice level.   None of this work could be appreciated by anyone's eye.   The inclinations contributed nothing to the view down the peristyle.   If a visitor had looked up at all (and Pausanias failed to, as he made no reference to the naos frieze in his description of the Parthenon) his eye would have been drawn to the carved frieze above the naos wall or to the detail of the coffering cut into the marble ceiling panels.   It has already been pointed out that Athenian builders of the time were particularly averse to expending unnecessary energy on tasks which had no aesthetical purpose.   They were willing and no doubt happy to elaborate stone with detail which would be seen and enjoyed, such as cutting an intricate string of bead and reel ornament, a mere 18mm in diameter, around the top of the external triglyphs and metope panels to link them together, however tenuously, but

121

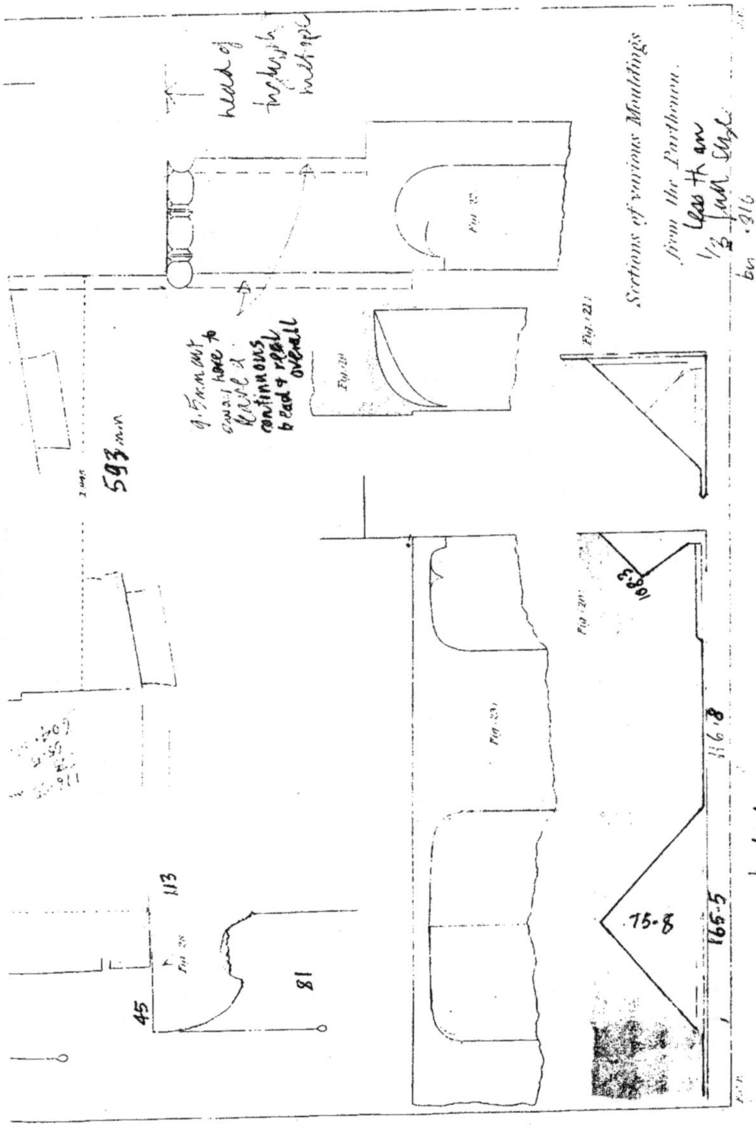

Fig. 49 THE BEAD AND REEL AT THE TOP OF THE TRIGLYPHS AND METOPES

there could have been no such purpose intended on the tedious working back of the internal face of the peristyle entablature without achieving any visual effect.   Why was it done?   There must have been a purpose.   What was it?   What was achieved? 79mm of extra width for the ceiling panels along the flanks is the only discernible benefit.   Why should that have been necessary? It was shown in (6) above that the ceiling panels had been cleverly designed to accommodate the unpredictability of the resultant width of the clear ceiling dimension by allowing the precise location of the bead and reel detail to be decided when the overall width of the ceiling was known.   If the overall width of the ceiling area had turned out to be 79mm wider than it now is, in other words, if the laborious adjustments had not been made to the inner faces of the Parthenon entablature, the bead and reel detail on the ceiling would have been cut 35mm from the coffers, leaving a border between them at mid span still equal to that at the edges, and no-one, either then or now, would have thought anything was amiss.   The only conclusion which can be drawn is that the ceiling panels had already been finished, complete with the bead and reel ornament, in sufficient quantities to warrant committing the workforce to the future labour of adjusting the entire length of both flanks of the inner face of the peristyle.   This mismatch of the ceiling width and the existing ceiling panels would have come to light in stage three of the building programme, when, if all the ceiling panels were to be new, only eight ceiling panels would need to be placed.   If all the ceiling panels were to be new, it is extremely unlikely that more than eight ceiling panels would have been finished so far ahead of need (stage four being by far the longest stage in the whole sequence) especially without knowing whether the dimension which was being assumed for the clear ceiling span was correct.

(12)   The unusual lengths of the external architrave beams over the peristyle.

The usual arrangement of a Greek Doric entablature has the joints between the lengths of architrave beams located over the centre lines of the pillars which support them, and the triglyphs, in the frieze course above, also placed directly over the pillars, as well as centrally between them.   On the Parthenon they were not arranged in this way.   On the only length of frieze recorded by Penrose the fifteen metopes of the east front, which determine the regularity or otherwise of the triglyph spacing, average 1.2785m wide, but only two are this width.   The rest range from 1.227m to 1.325m, a difference of 98mm, and contrary to what has been claimed,[3] they are not arranged in any systematic progression of width.   From the south they measure: 1.258m, 1.256m, 1.279m, 1.279m, 1.276m, 1.271m, 1.325m, 1.325m, 1.317m, 1.305m, 1.305m, 1.227m, 1.239m, 1.239m, and 1.277m at the north end.   Penrose also measured the Propylaia frieze, recording only two widths of metope, and they were within 6mm of each other.   The pillars beneath the frieze of the Parthenon east front deviate slightly from the average spacing in a sequence, -6mm, +2mm, +4mm, -4.5mm, and +5mm, showing that the irregular spacing of the triglyphs is not derived from the pillar spacing, as at least one writer has supposed.[4]

One of the new characteristics of the design of the Parthenon was the attempt to make all the pillar spacings in the fronts and the flanks equal.   The average spacing, apart from those at the corners, was:

---

[3] Dinsmoor A.A.G. p.162   *"A careful gradation from excessively wide metopes at the centre to narrow metopes towards the corners".*
[4] W.B.Dinsmoor Jr. review of Carpenter's 'Architects of the Parthenon' in A.J.A.75, p.339 - 340.

north	south	east	west
4.293m	4.294m	4.297m	4.297m

Within these sets of average dimensions there were variations,

on the north flank, ranging from	-30mm to +12mm
on the south flank, ranging from	-10mm to +16mm
on the east front, ranging from	-6mm to +5mm
on the west front, ranging from	-3mm to +3mm

Apart from a few on the flanks, these variations are remarkably slight, more than half of them being 5mm or less, and considering the size of stones being placed, the architect in charge of the work, if he was aware, would not have been concerned.   Contrary to commonly held opinion the variations of pillar spacing on the flanks had no effect on what was to happen above in the entablature, as will be shown. The triglyphs are not centred over pillars, by as much as 152mm and 91mm in places. What is equally strange, these displacements result in the longest beams, those at the ends, being longer by those amounts than they would need to be if 'canonical' arrangements had been followed.   Such apparently random beam lengths can have been arrived at only by a foreknowledge of which metope panel was to go where within the frieze arrangement, since all the metopes differed in width.   It was the normal practice to carve, on the architrave beams, regulae of the same width as the triglyphs to be placed above them in the frieze, and these regulae were given that description because it was understood that they regulated the relationship between the pillars and the elements of the frieze.   Masons, asked to make an architrave beam of a given length and height would, unless directed otherwise, and having been told the triglyph width to be used, cut half a regula at each end and one centrally between. Those working on the Parthenon must have been bemused to be told not to fix the position of the

Fig. 50 METOPE XXVI IN THE BRITISH MUSEUM

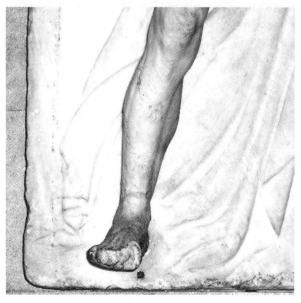

regulae on the main beams because they would be located afterwards; in this case it was the variable size of the metopes which would govern where the regulae would be!   And it was the irregular widths across the carved face of the metopes which determined how long any beam was to be made!   Rhys Carpenter has pointed out that of the fifteen metopes which are in the British Museum, numbers VII, VIII, XXV, XXX and XXXI have had the Kentaur's tail or hindquarters cut away or trimmed to allow the metope panel to fit into the groove cut in the sides of the triglyph stones to keep the metopes upright, and numbers XXVI and XXVII have had drapery cut away for the same purpose.   On his Plate 7, (see fig.35) Penrose, recording his measurements of the east front of the Parthenon, noted where a fifth of the north slant face of the fifth triglyph from the north-east corner is cut away to make room for the arm of a standing figure carved on the adjacent metope. A fifth of the horizontal shift of the slant face on the triglyph is about 16mm, and that the defacement of a finished triglyph was necessary to gain this slight amount, shows that without it the metope would have been unstable; there was not enough plain stone backing projecting beyond the carved figure   to enter the groove already cut in the side of the triglyph to receive it.   It is difficult to accept that weeks of labour would be lavished on the metope stone - over 1.3m square - if there had not been sufficient border material left at the sides to enable it to be readily used in the building it was being made to adorn.   Such a mistake made once in the whole building might have been understandable, but to find seven other instances out of fifteen which can be inspected, could imply that the metope spaces allowed in the 448 BC design of the Parthenon were not those for which the metope panels had been made, and that the originally wider metope stones had been reduced to fit into the smaller spaces left for them in a revised design.   Figure 50 shows how drapery in the bottom left corner was partially dressed away to allow the metope to fit the new location.

There can be alternative explanations of the displacement of triglyphs from their usual position in relation to the pillars; one, that in 448 BC the architects deliberately commissioned 92 metopes to be carved, all to different widths, with the many complications that were to ensue being foreseen and welcomed, or that the metopes had been commissioned and completed for an earlier design, where the notional space left for the metope panels was significantly larger than the specified width over the carving.   While Penrose reproduced the details of the triglyphs on his plate 20 (see fig.49), he made no reference in his text to the extraordinary use of the bead and reel ornament carved as a continuous band around the top of each triglyph and metope panel.   Being in the most vulnerable part of each frieze stone at the time when the cornice blocks were being placed, there would have been a high risk of damage to this detail, had not the undercutting on the face been carried out afterwards with all the stones in situ; (an excellent training ground for young masons, to give them experience in accuracy and lightness of touch in a situation where few, other than the master mason, would ever be aware of the results.)   This would suggest that the triglyphs of the earlier Parthenon may have been 18mm wider over the capping.   The Parthenon triglyph is the same width over the full height, below the bead and reel detail, although the whole cap projects forward at the front about 1.5mm.

(13)   The asymmetrical positioning of the architrave beams.

There is another unusual feature of the architrave beams on the Parthenon.   Penrose's dimensions on plate 6 (see fig.51) showed that they were set asymmetrically, front to rear, on the abacus of each pillar supporting them.   Penrose did not record the dis-

128

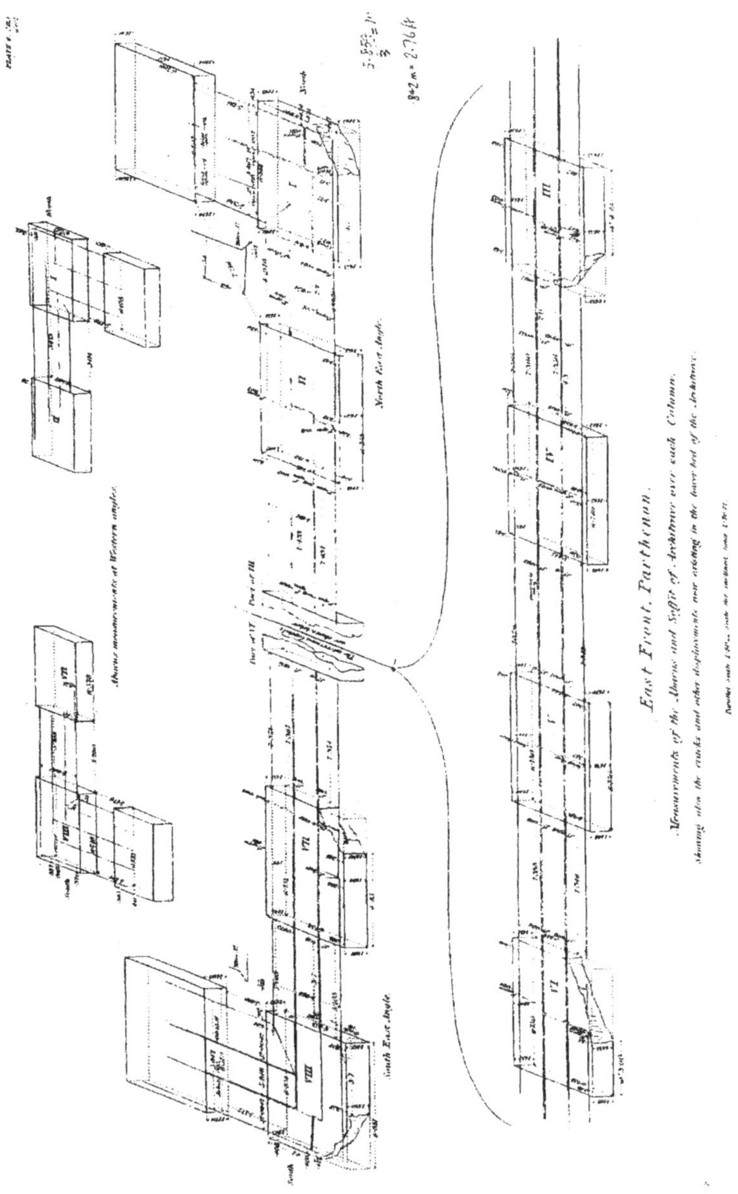

Fig. 51 PENROSE'S PLATE 6

placement of the beams in every case, presumably because the beams which survived on the flanks could not be assumed to have remained in their original positions during the explosion of 1687 which blew the rest away.   Where he recorded it most completely, at the east end, the difference between inside and outside measurements on the abacus is consistently in the range 64 to 67mm, and over the two pillars measured at the west end it is 57mm and 68mm.   Against this, the only two other places he dimensioned, one on the south flank and one on the west front, both next to the south-west corner, the displacement is only 12mm and 8mm on an average of two measurements in each case.

Other major buildings erected as part of the Periklean programme, such as the Hephaisteion and the Propylaia, invariably had beams which were centred on the pillars supporting them, as would be expected.   There must have been a sound reason for the beams being moved outwards in the case of the Parthenon, which was by far the largest and the most important of the Athenian structures of the period.   The accuracy of masonry technique displayed throughout the temple rules out the possibility of workmen's error.   The reason for the displacement of the beams is suggested by the amount of stone missing along the inward face of the architrave assembly.   In the architrave course three separate stones are set side by side to make up the width of the beam, and the outer one is cut at the top with a continuous band, the taenia, beneath which at intervals are the regulae with their guttae hanging from them; these line up with triglyphs in the frieze course above.   Penrose's Plate 22 (see fig.53) illustrated this detail to scale.   The projection of the taenia is 67mm, and the diameter of the round guttae is 69mm.   This is the minimum amount of stone which would have to be cut away in order to re-use the stone from an earlier temple.   It appears that these beams, like the metopes,

Fig. 52 SECTIONS SHOWING DISPLACEMENT OF ARCHITRAVE BEAMS

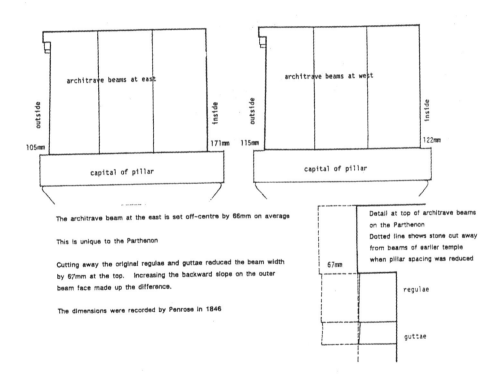

architrave beams at east

outside

inside

105mm   171mm

capital of pillar

architrave beams at west

outside

inside

115mm   122mm

capital of pillar

The architrave beam at the east is set off-centre by 66mm on average

This is unique to the Parthenon

Cutting away the original regulae and guttae reduced the beam width by 67mm at the top.   Increasing the backward slope on the outer beam face made up the difference.

The dimensions were recorded by Penrose in 1846

67mm

Detail at top of architrave beams on the Parthenon
Dotted line shows stone cut away from beams of earlier temple when pillar spacing was reduced

regulae

guttae

Fig. 53 DETAIL OF REGULAE AND GUTTAE ON THE PARTHENON

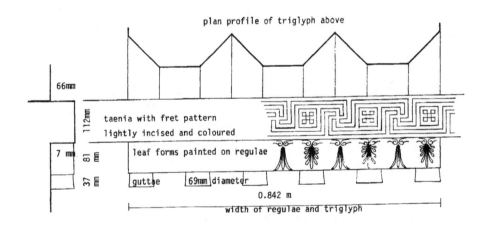

had been intended for an earlier structure with different pillar spacing. Penrose recorded the overall width of the beam at the seating level in each case.   He also recorded on Plates 7 and 8 (see figs.35 and 36) the backward sloping profile of the main outer face of the beam by taking offsets from a plumb line.   The beam face slopes back towards the top by 16mm.   Although there is no way of knowing whether the beams to be used on the earlier Parthenon were designed to have a backward sloping face on the outside, adding a slope or increasing it when it came to be re-cut, would have been a labour-saving way of keeping the width of beam as great as possible at its bearing surface.   It is difficult to think of any explanation for the displaced seating of these major elements, and their erratic lengths, other than that they were re-fashioned for use on a structure whose pillar centres had been reduced below those for which the beams were originally cut.   The projecting detail at the top of the outer beam would have had to be dressed off and the entire face of the beam cut again to suit the requirements of altered metope widths to be placed above.   The bulk of this work would have been done at ground level, by cutting three receding planes, one below the other at the top of the stone, with the new taenia running the entire length of the beam.   When the revised length had been calculated the two half regulae, one at each end and the central one, would be approximately defined for position along the beam. The final cutting of the detail below the taenia would only have been carried out when the frieze elements above it were all in place to the satisfaction of the architect.   The metopes on the Parthenon had to be finally slid into position sideways, not simply lowered in from above, because the projecting carving was now too near the triglyphs, as Penrose's observation had confirmed, and would not have cleared the corner of the triglyph capping.

There is another detail recorded by Penrose which supports this suggested explanation. It is shown on his plates 6 and 7. Plate 6 (see fig.51) shows how the outer of the three stones making up the architrave beam at the corners of the temple had to be cut from much wider stones than the rest to form, in plan view, an 'L' shaped return of stone at the corner. The extra labour involved was immense. A stone 1.4m high, over 5m long and nearly 1m thick had to be won from the quarry and hauled to the site. The shaping of it, to the required finished dimensions, entailed cutting away almost a third of its thickness over all of its height and most of its length in order to leave an exposed width at the end equal to the triglyph width above, enabling the regula below the taenia on the return face at the corner to be cut from a single stone. The intended detail, carried out in the traditional way, can be seen on the Hephaisteion and on the north-west and south-west corners of the Parthenon, where one of the extra new beams required for the enlarged temple could be worked as originally intended There would be no point in bringing a stone from the quarry which was substantially thicker than necessary, unless it could be worked to a finished width of 0.849m at one end; half regulae could otherwise have been accepted here as they were over every other pillar, apart from those at the corners. But Penrose's drawing of the return face of this east front beam showed it on plate 7 (see fig.35) to be 0.774m wide. The width of the rest of the beam, along the east front is 0.539m. At the return end, it is a mere 75mm short of its desired width. We have seen that the minimum amount of stone to be dressed off the face of the architrave beam, in order to make it re-usable, was 67mm. At the return face, this was not enough to be cut away; a little more needed to be removed from the L shaped return face to place the joint with the next architrave beam on the flank clear of the last guttae of the six, an undercut form which could not be safely made to straddle a joint between two stones.

Fig. 54 RETURN FACE OF FRONT ARCHITRAVES ON THE FLANKS

Corner—Hephaisteion.

North east corner Parthenon
showing old beam re-used.

South West corner Parthenon
showing new beam used.

Was this merely a slavish adherence to tradition pursued by Athenian builders? With temples of the scale of the Hephaisteion and the earlier Temple of Aphaia on Aigina, where elements of the structure are half the size of those on the Parthenon, such a detail at the corner would have been a desirable way of terminating the end beam of the front architrave. The doubling of the size of each dimension was embarked upon without any consideration of an alternative way of resolving the awkward implications at the ends of the corner architrave beams. Rather than laboriously form an enlargement at the end, it would have been very simple to reduce the width of the front element so that the joint with the adjoining beam on the flank of the temple occurred in the centre of the corner triglyph, like every other architrave joint. After all, the technique of anathyrosis was intended to disguise the vertical joint. Neither the architect of the earlier Parthenon nor his successor considered doing this, even when the latter had to order new extra beams for the west end of his enlarged design. It seems that the Athenian temple builders practised the principle defined later by Ruskin as the 'Lamp of Sacrifice'; labour itself was offered up to the gods.[5] However, Iktinos was prepared to compromise at the east end where the original beams - no longer having an adequately long return face, the front face having been cut back to accommodate the closer spacing of the triglyphs, had to be adjusted to suit the spacing of the guttae. Presumably the pressing need for a speedy completion of the project and considerations of cost were beginning to be crucial.

Why did Penrose decline to draw attention in his text to these anomalies of placement and detail on the beams? They must have registered in his mind, but because the interest of his

---

[5] John Ruskin 'The Seven Lamps of Architecture' 1849. Ruskin would never have acknowledged that the authors of classical architecture knew sacrifice in this sense.

published work was directed towards optical refinements in Athenian architecture, and these were features which could not be so described, he left them unremarked. We tend to see only what we are looking for. His immediate preoccupation was directed elsewhere. We are grateful nevertheless that he published his findings in such detail that, while he himself must have been puzzled at what he had discovered, he did not suppress it merely because it did not contribute to his main thesis.

(14)   Other indications of the re-use of building elements.

The remaining evidence that the Parthenon was composed of re-cycled elements is twofold; a hint in the Parthenon building accounts for the first year, themselves fragmentary, and also, by inference only, from Vitruvius's 'De Architectura'.

Dinsmoor   summarised his reconstruction of the Parthenon building accounts for Year 1 447/6 BC. to confirm,

> *"Payments were made for quarrying and transporting marble (though not yet for working it), for wages of carpenters and labourers, and for salaries of the epistatae, architects, and secretaries."*

This is a strong indication that masons were not employed, although carpenters and labourers were. According to the accepted scenario for this year, a new stylobate would have had to be set out and made, a process requiring masons to work stone, either new or reclaimed from undamaged sections of what was there before. Until this was in place and stones for the pillar drums were also partially shaped by masons and ready for lifting into position, there would be little need for carpenters. Some sleds for moving the stylobate stones from the unloading bay to where they were to be worked would have been required, but this would not be a contract of a scale worthy of mention. However, if work had slowed down or stopped altogether on a temple which was almost completed, then carpenters and labourers would have been needed in large numbers, to erect and dismantle scaffolding, take the stone structure apart under the direction of the architects, and move the pieces on sleds to where they could be stored in an orderly sequence for re-use. This process would have taken about two years, allowing for the fact that, in dismantling, the crane would not need to be moved to a new station after every lift, but could stay in one location, for instance, while the whole of a pillar was being taken down. Future work on the Parthenon building accounts may bring to light more evidence of what was recorded as having taken place in the first three years.

It may be significant that the only reference we have of what must surely be the most important work ever written about the Parthenon is recorded by a Roman engineer, Marcus Vitruvius Pollio, who offered to his emperor Augustus Caesar, around 25 BC., his own treatise, 'De Architectura'. In the introduction to Book VII he included in his list of architectural descriptions written by ancients, one by *"Ictinus and Carpion, on the Doric temple of Minerva which is on the acropolis of Athens"*, without telling us anything of its contents. We know that Iktinos was one of the architects of the Parthenon so, whether or not Karpion assisted in an architectural role, their book must have been an account of the building being erected by Iktinos. Even at the time, therefore, the building of the temple for Athene was considered to be a protracted event which deserved a record being made of it in words. Evidently the form of the building itself was not thought to provide the information which the words were employed to convey. What could that have been? We know from Penrose how complex and atypical the Parthenon

Fig. 55 DORIC ORDER ACCORDING TO VITRUVIUS

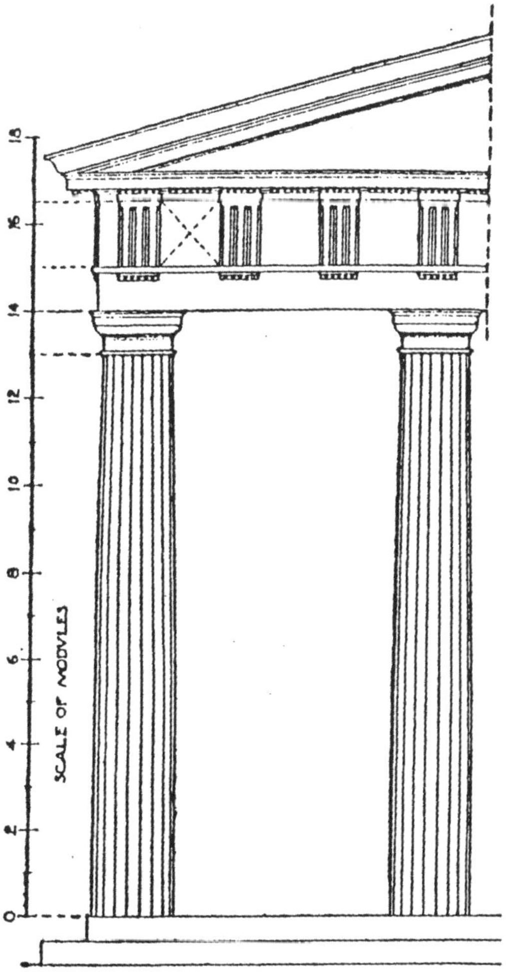

is as an example of Greek Doric architecture of that time, but was it the unusual character of the building that was described in the book written by Iktinos and Karpion?   If so, there is nothing in Vitruvius's treatise to show that he had ever read it, or, if he had, valued what it may have said about the architecture.   The Roman's text exhibits no knowledge or understanding of the Parthenon.   In it he recommended for builders wishing to build in the Doric style, a system of proportions which results in buildings bearing no relationship to anything the Greeks of the time had built in Athens, or anything which could have been described in the Greek book.   Could it be that the only significance of the Greek book for Vitruvius and for his Roman contemporaries, and his reason for mentioning it to his emperor, was that it described in detail how a large temple like the Parthenon could be taken apart, stone by stone, and re-erected in a larger form?   Certainly one of the other texts referred to by Vitruvius, that by Theodoros describing the Temple of Hera on Samos, had technical features which would have interested an engineer, such as the reinforcing of swampy ground in order to extend the foundation, and the use of a lathe, invented by Theodoros, to turn the round pillars of stone.

It is at least a coincidence that, in the last two decades of the first century BC., a time when the book written by Iktinos and Karpion was still known, and after Vitruvius had drawn his attention to it, Augustus embarked on a programme of dismantling Greek temples and moving them, or parts of them, to other sites.   The most notable of these was the temple of Ares, which had been originally a part of Perikles's temple building programme between 448 and 432 BC., erected probably at

140

Pallene,[6] and brought piece by piece to the agora of a diminished Athens, to be re-erected there around 14 BC.

---

[6] For many years the original site was thought to be at Akharnai, but a foundation discovered at Pallene is the same size as that required for the temple moved to the Agora.

STUDY 4   THE DESIGN OF THE EARLIER PARTHENON

Study 1 showed that, after an understandable lapse of time following the departure from Athens of the Persian occupying army, work on the project to build a new temple for Athene was resumed.   The huge wall built in the 460's is evidence that the master plan, initiated by Aristeides and his contemporaries, to extend the Akropolis site and cover up those parts of the foundation for the new temple which were never intended to be seen, had been taken up by Kimon with the intention of implementing it.   Studies 2 and 3 have shown how Penrose's drawings of his survey of the Parthenon remains in 1846-7 revealed not only how the temple was built but also the probable extensive re-use of elements of an earlier Parthenon design in its construction.

B.H.Hill's paper 'The Older Parthenon', published in 1912, listed the components of an earlier design for the Parthenon which remained at the time when he wrote his paper.   He understood all of them to have been parts of a pre-Persian-occupation temple in course of construction when Xerxes's army returned in 480BC.   It is more likely that some of them, such as the naos step stones cut from Pentelic marble, referred to in Study 2, were from a post-Persian and pre-Perikleian earlier structure, otherwise they could not have been found to be placed twice in their useful life; the pre-Persian- occupation temple construction could not have been sufficiently advanced to have allowed their use at that time.

Can the other remains, those not modified and adapted for re-use in the Parthenon, tell us anything about the design of the earlier Parthenon?   They consist of the following elements: pillar drums, orthostate course wall blocks, steps, stylobate blocks, and moulded wall-base blocks.

(1)   Pillar drums.

Penrose showed that pillar drums of the earlier Parthenon differed from those of the Parthenon only in having a more refined flute profile at the very bottom, matching the form of that on the pillar capitals found on the Parthenon.   Their bottom surface would have been shaped to fit slopes on the pavement different from those of the later Parthenon, resulting from the shallower curve on the top surface of the earlier stylobate blocks upon which they were to sit, a surface which would have been parallel to that of the podium platform.

(2)   Orthostate course wall blocks.

The fragments of orthostate blocks remaining in an unfinished state must be from stones which had suffered accidental damage either in the course of being made, or which had been erected into the fabric of the resumed construction of the earlier Parthenon and, being taken down for re-use, were damaged in the process.

(3)   Steps.

The re-used stones found in the lower course of steps below the naos walls of the later Parthenon were thought by Hill to come mostly from the lower of two naos steps of the earlier temple, although he acknowledged that the evidence for a second step on this earlier temple was not strong.[1]   M. Korres, in his recon-

---

[1] B.H.Hill, 'The Older Parthenon' A.J.A. vol.XVI 1912 p.551n1 .

struction plan of the earlier Parthenon,[2] has relied heavily on Hill but showed only one step.   If this were the case, one step would have allowed enough height for a full Doric frieze to be built over pro-naos pillars, similar to those found on the Parthenon, in the same situation within the earlier Parthenon. (see fig.46).

The major triumph of Hill's 1912 paper was his clarification of the role, in the design of the earlier Parthenon, of the Kara limestone blocks forming the lowest step of the earlier krepidoma.   He accounted for about fifty of these stones built in the north wall of the Akropolis, on some of which a setting line could still be detected which indicated another stone was to be placed above them leaving part of the Kara stone exposed as a step intended to be 0.673m wide when finished.   Other Kara stones had been discovered within the Parthenon perimeter step construction behind the corresponding steps of the later structure.   Dörpfeld had supposed these to be Kara stylobate stones placed above steps made of the same stone used in the construction of the foundation platform.   Hill established that the earlier Parthenon had a marble stylobate and a marble step built over a bottom step of Kara limestone,[3] all of which were set to the same degree of upward curve as the foundation platform surface.

Penrose had drawn attention to the similarity of this curve to that found on the stylobate of the Hephaisteion.   It is also interesting to note that on that temple, built in the mid-5th century, the lowest of the steps to the temple is made, not of

---

[2] M.Korres 'From Pentelicon to the Parthenon' fig. 35.1 on p.112.

[3] This feature, of the lowest step of the krepidoma being cut from a darker stone than the two steps above, was a design ploy which persisted in Athens from the earliest years of the 5th. century well into the 430's, notably in the Hephaisteion and on the west front of the Propylaia, and is evidence of a school of design well established in the building trade throughout those years.

white marble like the rest of the structure, but of a darker stone; these are two stylistic links across nearly forty years which must have some explanation, in the light of both being disregarded by the architect of the later Perikleian Parthenon.   The Kara step stone at the extreme south-west of the earlier Parthenon was a corner stone and its position reflected the mid-5th century rebuilding of the Temple of Poseidon at Sounion in being not only raised up on a base foundation, but also set back from the edge of it to leave a walk-way around the outside of the peristyle and krepidoma.

Other remaining blocks of Pentelic marble, which clearly had been steps, having setting lines marked on them for the stones to be placed above, were also found in or near the north wall of the Akropolis. Fragments of marble steps, identified by Hill as being from corner blocks, indicated exposed widths of tread of 0.667m on the flanks and 0.679m on the fronts of the earlier temple, measured on the intermediate marble step.   From these step widths Hill claimed to arrive at his estimate of the overall dimensions of the temple. It was in determining the overall dimensions of the stylobate level above these steps that Hill departed from reason and based his supposed dimensions of the temple on an assumption that it was placed centrally on the foundation platform, the sizes of which could be measured.   He knew that the Kara stone nearest to the south and the west was a corner stone, and was able to establish that it was still in its original position by observing that the stone on which it was placed had been cut away some 20mm deep immediately to the south edge of it (this cutting also leaving some accidental scars on the Kara stone itself).   The cutting was to provide a new bed level for the marble step of the later Parthenon, one set to a more pronounced vertical curve (see fig.38) which had later been placed 200mm in front of it.   He assumed that the distances at which this Kara limestone block was set from both the west,

145

3.6m, and from the south, 2.6m, edges of the foundation platform were repeated at the east and the north edges of the original platform area. From this assumption Hill proceeded to devise a pattern of pillar spacings to fit the resultant stylobate dimensions. The overall dimensions of the platform foundation were given by Penrose as the equivalent of 31.778m x 76.9m, and by Hill as 31.39m x 76.816m, with a vagueness as to where the front dimension was measured. Penrose showed the top course of the platform cut back along some of the east front and most of the south side, leaving a shelf about 0.45m wide. This feature seems to have confused Dörpfeld into thinking it was part of an original stepped base for a temple with a stylobate of Kara marble. However the distance of the cutting back from the face of the platform increased abruptly and substantially below the space between the 5th and 6th later Parthenon pillars from the west end, roughly where Stage One of the construction of the pre-Persian earlier Parthenon would have ended.(see fig.45) This would suggest that the original edge of this top course also suffered severe fire damage at the west end, as could be expected, the majority of the scaffolding having been erected there. During any resumed building of the earlier Parthenon design in the 460's the intention would have been to restore the top course of the foundation to its original profile on completion of the work on the temple. On the south side this appeared as a header course, that is, with the shorter dimension of each stone showing to the south; the plan would have been to edge it with longer and probably broader stones. As things turned out, the architect of the later Parthenon decided to hide the whole of the foundation by raising the ground level even higher. The upper course of the foundation was then cut into to form the greater degree of curvature required for the marble steps and stylobate of the later Parthenon. An extra, shallow step was introduced below the krepidoma to set the new level of paving to the terrace beyond the three marble steps. (See fig.45)

146

(4)   Stylobate blocks.

It may have seemed to be a reasonable assumption that the earlier Parthenon would have been sited centrally on the foundation platform, had not Hill reported in the same paper the sizes and description of marble stylobate blocks which had survived from the earlier temple.   These stones were of two kinds.   Some were fire damaged and were found built into the north wall of the Akropolis immediately above the fire damaged pillar base stones also removed from the temple, a sequence which suggests that the transferences were made as part of a single operation.   These stones, like others, had been cut in two for ease of manhandling, presumably by workmen acting on the instruction of Themistokles to strengthen the north boundary, thought to be insecure after its suspected breach by Persian troops.   Four others, still at full size, had been later built into the structure extending the foundation platform at the north-west corner, required to support the widened Parthenon.   Two others were built uncut into the north boundary wall.   When Hill was writing, one full size stylobate block was still lying near the Akropolis Museum which had been built to house the artifacts rescued from the site excavation.

Some of these stones were measured by Hill's young associate W.B. Dinsmoor, drawn and reproduced as Figure 11 in Hill's 1912 paper.(see fig.56)   They showed traces of the shallow circular sinking cut into the upper surface to receive the pillar base stones.   By superimposing concentrically, within this line, the fluted outline from a pillar base of the earlier Parthenon found nearby, Dinsmoor had established that on this original version of the temple the pillars, with an overall diameter of 1.903m, stood centrally on one stone of the stylobate and overlapped on to the edges of the two adjacent blocks. Since the adjoining edges of these blocks were worked to a finished line,

Fig. 56 B.H. HILL'S FIG. 11 DESCRIBING STYLOBATE STONES OF THE EARLIER
PARTHENON

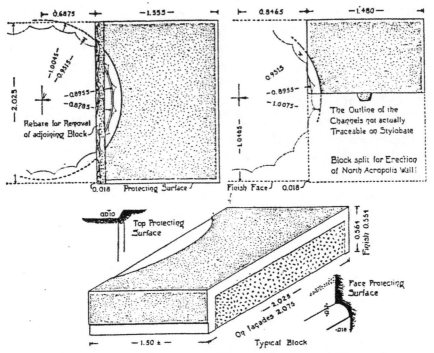

FIGURE 11. — DETAILS OF MARBLE STYLOBATE BLOCKS.[1]

Fig. 57 LAYOUT OF STYLOBATE STONES AT THE WEST END COMPARED

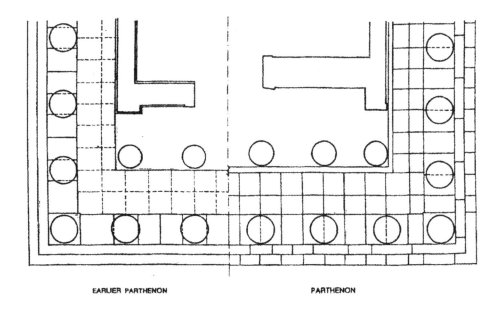

EARLIER PARTHENON   PARTHENON

the distance of the stylobate joint located between the pillars and the centre of the pillars could be known. The information on Hill's Figure 11 showed two different pillar spacings. It might be thought that the measured stones may not have come from the general run of the stylobate but from the corners, where the pillar spacing would be atypic, but reference to figure 57, a reconstruction of the sort of corner arrangement that would follow from these stylobate stone dimensions, shows that this is unlikely. Rather the dimensions can be interpreted as the standard spacings of the pillars of the earlier Parthenon on the fronts - 4.653m - and on the flanks - 4.485m. These surviving stones also showed that the margin outside the full diameter of the pillars, measured to the finished stylobate edge would have been 97mm. In combination, these pillar spacings can be shown to have an arithmetical integrity which is missing from those devised by both Hill and Dinsmoor.

(5)   Questionable nature of the dimensions used by Hill and Dinsmoor.

From his assumption of the centrality of the location of the temple on its foundation B.H.Hill had arrived at stylobate dimensions of 23.51m x 66.888m. In combination with his assessment of pillar spacings of 4.53m on the fronts and 4.4m on the flanks, these dimensions give rise to spacings at the corners of 3.891m on the fronts and 3.77m on the flanks. Because of the arrangement of a Doric frieze, pillar spacings at the corners are always less than the rest but these would be large reductions from the standard spacings, rivalling those on the fronts and exceeding those on the flanks of the later Parthenon, which are themselves extreme. W.B.Dinsmoor must have had his own reservations about Hill's calculations as he published in 1950 his own ideas about the dimensions of the earlier Parthenon. While retaining the notion of the central siting of the temple, he revised the size of the stylobate to 23.533m x 66.94m.   The pillar spacings he devised are in the table below, where the earlier Parthenon is referred to as O.P.(for Older Parthenon, the name used by both Hill and Dinsmoor)

Reductions of corner pillar spacings compared						
	standard front	corner front	% reduction	standard flank	corner flank	% reduction
Hill O.P.	4.53m	3.891m	14.1	4.4m	3.77m	14.32
Parthenon	4.297m	3.683m	14.29	4.293m	3.697m	13.883
Dinsmoor O.P.	4.413m	4.08m	7.546	4.359m	4.0645m	6.756
Hephaisteion	2.583m	2.413m	6.58	2.581m	2.413m	6.509
T.of Ares	2.69m	2.53m	5.948	2.69m	2.53m	5.948
T.of Poseidon Sounion	2.522m	2.374m	5.868	2.522m	2.374m	5.868
T.of Aphaia Aigina	2.618m	2.4m	8.327	2.5605m	2.327	9.12
T.of Athene (Peisistratid)	4.042m	3.732m	7.67	3.834m	3.467m	9.572

It is difficult to comprehend how both Hill and Dinsmoor arrived at their pillar spacings for the earlier Parthenon since neither declared the width they had assumed for the triglyph.   Because there was an even number of metopes and an odd number of triglyphs in a Greek Doric frieze, the width of the triglyph relative to that of the metope makes a marginal difference to the overall length of any frieze supported by the pillars in relation to the length of the stylobate on which the pillars stand.   For this reason scholars have found it convenient to adopt the rule promulgated by Vitruvius nearly 500 years after the earlier Parthenon was designed, that metopes should be 1.5 times the width of the triglyph.   While this has the virtue of simplicity, it should never be assumed as holy writ where 5th century Athenians have been involved.

Penrose measured the Doric remains of the Propylaia, the Parthenon and two lengths of frieze from a 6th century temple destroyed by the Persians and, after 480BC., built into the north wall of the Akropolis.   The ratio of metope to triglyph width which he recorded for the Propylaia were 1.576:1 and 1.567:1, and for the Parthenon, because the metopes are not a constant width, they range between 1.574:1 and 1.458:1, averaging 1.518:1.   With the group built into the north wall located towards the east being 1.53:1 and 1.44:1, and the group towards the west 1.55:1 and 1.56:1, they indicate a refreshing freedom from dogma on such matters persisting on the Akropolis of Athens from 530 to about 440BC., the approximate dates within which these examples would have been designed, according to Dinsmoor's own chronological list of Greek temples.   It is still possible that the ratio employed on the earlier Parthenon could have been precisely 1.5:1.

From this assumption metope and triglyph widths can be calculated because the space between pillar centres (S) = 2 x metope width (M) + 2 x triglyph width (T) and M = 1.5T. Hill's dimensions would have made the frieze length equal the stylobate length on both front and flank, an unusual circumstance resulting, if the pillars were similar to those of the later Parthenon at the top as they were at the bottom, in their leaning outward 150mm on the fronts and 142mm along the flanks.[4]   Substituting the Parthenon width of triglyph in Hill's

---

[4]   Calculation of Hill's corner spacings resulting from his standard pillar spacings and his assumed stylobate dimensions.

On the front:	stylobate width	= 23.51m
Minus standard space (4.53m) x 3		= 13.59m
Minus corner pillar diameter (1.944m) + 2 x margin (0.097m)		= 2.138m
Corner pillar spacing is 7.782 / 2 = 3.891m		
On the flank: similarly, where standard spacing is 4.4m and stylobate is 66.88m		
Corner pillar spacing is	3.770m	*Cont'd*

dimensions would reduce the amount of outward lean to 131mm on the fronts and 140mm on the flanks.   Dinsmoor's dimensions would have made the pillars lean inwards by excessive amounts, 190mm on the fronts and 145mm on the flanks, increased to 204mm on the fronts and 161mm on the flanks if the Parthenon size of triglyph had been used.[5]

Calculation of lean on the pillars resulting from Hill's dimensions for pillar spacings, his assumed Stylobate sizes and assuming T:M = 1:1.5

With front pillar spacing   4.53m   then T =   0.906m   and M =   1.359m
Front frieze   =   11 x T + 10 x M   = 23.556m (Hill stylobate =   23.51m)
With flank pillar spacing 4.40m then T = 0.880m   and M =   1.320m
Flank frieze   =   31 x T + 30 x M = 66.880m (Hill stylobate = 66.888m)

Front frieze length   23.556m
Adding 2 x margin (0.125m) to abacus edge and subtracting abacus width,
 + 0.250m – 2.090m   =   21.716m (c/1 to c/1 pillars at frieze)
    3 x 4.53m + 2 x 3.891m   =   21.372m (c/1 to c/1 corner pillars on stylobate)
Lean on pillars is   0.300m/2   =   142mm outward on the flanks

Flank frieze length   66.880m
Adding 2 x margin (0.125m) to abacus edge and subtracting the abacus width,
 + 0.250m – 2.090m   =   65.040m (c/1 to c/1 corner pillars at frieze)
    13 x 4.4m + 2 x 3.77m =   64.740m (c/1 to c/1 corner pillars on stylobate)
Lean on pillars is   0.300m/2   =   150mm outward on the fronts

If Hill had assumed T to be 0.8418m on front and flank, as on the Parthenon, then the ratios of T:M would have been 1:1.69 on the front and 1:1.613 on the flank and the outward lean would have been 140mm on the flanks and 131mm at the fronts.

[5] Calculation of lean on the pillars resulting from Dinsmoor's dimensions for pillar spacings, his assumed stylobate sizes and assuming T:M = 1:1.5

With front pillar spacing   4.413m,   then T =   0.8825m   and M =   1.324m
Front frieze   =   11 x T + 10 x M = 22.948m (Dinsmoor stylobate =   23.533m)
With flank pillar spacing   4.359m,   then T =   0.8718m   and M =   1.3077m
Flank frieze =   31 x T + 30 x M = 66.257m (Dinsmoor stylobate =   66.94m)

Front frieze length   22.948m
Adding 2 x margin (0.125m) to abacus edge and subtracting the abacus width,
 + 0.250m – 2.090m   =   21.109m (c/1 to c/1 corner pillars at frieze)
    3 x 4.413m + 2 x 4.080m   =   21.399m (c/1 to c/1 corner pillars on stylobate)
Lean on pillars is   0.290m/2   =   145mm at the flanks

Cont'd

Alternatively, the adjoining friezes sat on the corner capitals with very different margins to the abacus on front and flank.

The same analyses applied to the dimensions of pillar spacing measured by Dinsmoor from the archaeological evidence of the surviving stylobate stones of the earlier Parthenon, and the understanding that the Parthenon triglyphs had survived from the earlier temple, as had the metopes, the pillars and the architrave beams, delivers the proper equal relationship of frieze to corner pillar on both front and flank, suggesting that the amount of inward lean on each facade would have been the same.

(6)   The relationship of the Parthenon to the Temple of Aphaia on Aigina.

In arriving at the overall stylobate size of the earlier Parthenon derived from the original stylobate stones, it has been assumed that the degree of inward lean is exactly the same as that on the pillars of the Temple of Aphaia on Aigina.   Fürtwangler and others had measured these pillars in 1906 to be half the height of those on the Parthenon and leaning inwards 25mm.   Greek architects almost always built on their recent past.   In 488BC, when design work was beginning on the new temple for Athene

---

Flank frieze length		66.257m
Adding 2 x margin (0.125m) to abacus edge and subtracting the abacus width,		
+ 0.250 – 2.090m =		64.417m (c/1 to c/1 corner pillars at frieze)
13 x 4.359m + 2 x 4.0645m	=	64.796m (c/1 to c/1 corner pillars on stylobate)
Lean on pillars is 0.379m/2	=	189.5mm on the fronts

If Dinsmoor had assumed T to be 0.8418m on the front and flank, as on the Parthenon, then the ratio of T:M would have been 1:1.62 on the front and 1:1.59 on the flank, and the inward lean on the pillars would have been 161mm on the flanks and 204mm at the fronts.

on the Athenian Akropolis, this temple on Aigina, only 15 miles out from Phaleron, the port of Athens, was newly finished. Scholars have drawn attention to design links which may exist between Aigina and Attika.   The architect of the Temple of Aphaia on Aigina is not known by name, but the slenderness of the temple's pillars, with the height 5.33 times the base diameter, brings to mind those of the Athenian Treasury at Delphi, built about the same time.   J.J. Coulton has pointed out the extraordinary measures taken there to widen the narrow space between the two pillars at the entrance, including a slenderness ratio of 5.55:1 on the pillars, which might suggest that the Aphaia architect had a hand in its design.   M.M. Miles has observed that at Rhamnous there is one capital remaining from an earlier temple destroyed by the Persians which bears a strong similarity to those on the Temple of Aphaia, so the same architect may have been involved there too.   If the Athenians were looking for advice on how to set about building a new temple to commemorate their victory at Marathon, they could well have looked to the architects currently working on Aigina for it.   The aristocratic patrons of those times who were bright enough to commission Pindar to celebrate their athletic heroes would have ensured that the best talents available would have been employed to design their temples.

The Temple of Aphaia on Aigina had introduced a number of features which were found by Penrose on the Parthenon.   Pillars were made the same diameter on the front as on the flank, apart from those at the corners, which were made slightly fatter.   The architrave beams sat on the pillar capitals at Aigina much nearer to the edge than had been the practice earlier; they no longer lined up with the narrow neck of the pillars.   The angle of slope of the echinus, the circular moulding beneath the square abacus, was made steeper, transferring the load to the pillar more effectively as well as appearing to grow more elegantly out of the shaft.   The decision in 488 BC to build the new temple to Athene on the Athenian Akropolis with Pentelic marble would have encouraged the steepening of the echinus profile still further to keep the overall size of the huge capitals as small as possible.   Fürtwangler recorded the triglyph width on the Temple of Aphaia only on the front, presumably because it was no different on the flanks.   The metope widths would have differed only 30mm between the flank and the front where the pillar spacing was slightly larger.   The same principle was carried through the design of the later Parthenon, where all the triglyphs were the same width of 0.8418m, except at the corners where the linking of the end splays increased this to 0.849m, so it would not be unreasonable to think that a constant triglyph width would have been employed on the earlier Parthenon.

(7)   The basis for establishing the main dimensions of the earlier Parthenon.

If that was the case, then metope widths of 1.485m on the fronts and 1.401m on the flanks would govern the spacing of the corner pillars from their neighbours.   The greater width of metope on the front would have been seen as an advantage if they were to be carved.   These dimensions would result in corner pillar spacings on the earlier Parthenon which can be compared with those on the preceding table on page 151.

	std. front	corner front	% reduction	std flank	corner flank	% reduction
O.P. from stylobate blocks	4.653m	4.204m	9.65	4.485m	4.0365m	10

The archaeological evidence for the pillar diameters and the margin left beyond the pillars at the stylobate edge, combined with the pillar spacings from the same source shows the dimensions of the stylobate of the earlier Parthenon to have been 24.506m x 68.537m.[6]

Penrose measured the overall size of the original podium platform as 31.778m x 76.900m, whereas Dinsmoor recorded it as 31.390m x 76.816m.   There could be several explanations of the discrepancy, but since Penrose showed such painstaking accuracy in the rest of his recording, and illustrated exactly where his measurements applied, his dimensions have been taken here as being correct.   The temple peristyle plan defined

---

[6] Calculation of stylobate sizes resulting from spacing dimensions revealed by the earlier Parthenon stylobate stones and assuming T = 0.8418m as on the Parthenon.

Assuming there is no lean on the pillars.

With front pillar spacing 4.653m and T = 0.8418m, then M = 1.485m
Front frieze = 11 x T + 10 x M =   24.108m
Add 2 x margin (0.125m) to abacus edge and subtract abacus width (2.090m) (average of north-east and south-east sizes)
c/l to c/l of corner pillars at the capitals would be   22.268m
   subtracting 3 x standard pillar spacings   13.959m
remainder of 8.309m / 2 = 4.1545m would be the corner pillar spacing at the level of the capitals.
Adding 50mm for the amount of lean would make stylobate width on fronts
(3 x 4.653m) + (2 x 4.2045m) + 2.138m (2 x margin + corner pillar
diameter) =   24.506m

With flank pillar spacing 4.485m and T = 0.8418m, then M = 1.4007m
Flank frieze = 31 x T + 10 x M =   68.118m
Add 2 x margin (0.125m) to abacus edge and subtract abacus width (2.0685m) (average of south-east and south-west sizes)
c/l to c/l of corner pillars at the capitals would be   66.2995m
   subtracting 13 x standard pillar spacings   58.305m
remainder of 7.9945m / 2 = 3.997m would be the corner pillar spacing at the level of the capitals.
Adding 50mm for the amount of lean would make stylobate length on flanks
(13 x 4.485m + (2 x 4.047m + 2.138m (2 x margin + corner pillar
diameter =   68.537m

by these dimensions would have placed the pre-Persian earlier Parthenon on the podium with slightly more space left at the west (3.6m) and south (2.6m) sides, with the space at the east (2.059m) being made similar to that on the north flank (1.992m), rather than the west end as Hill had assumed.

The location of the new temple for Athene started in the 480's was complicated by the presence of an ancient shrine, the foundation of which existed where the north side of the podium for the temple met the natural rock of the Akropolis ridge. This would have determined the line of the northern edge of the earlier krepidoma. It was probably the presence of the same shrine site which required the drastic revision of the pillar spacing on the later Parthenon, to allow the shrine to be rebuilt within the north peristyle of the Perikleian version of the temple. The shrine would not have been rebuilt while the earlier Parthenon was still in course of construction.

(8)   The Parthenon and its predecessor share a common ceiling panel module.

Along the flanks, the earlier Parthenon can be shown to have had a ceiling length of 64.167m derived from the stylobate length of 68.537m.   On his plate 16 (see fig.37), Penrose gave enough dimensions to establish that the end of the ceiling of the Parthenon was set in from the edge of the stylobate 2.096m. This would have been 2.006m on the earlier Parthenon before the margin between the pillars and the edge of the stylobate, the lean on the pillars and the inner face of the peristyle entablature were altered on the later version.   The resulting ceiling length on the earlier Parthenon was equal to 52 modules, each of 1.234m, allowing for the return of a full margin of 0.342m around the coffers at each end.   Penrose had measured the ceiling module on the Parthenon, from fragments of one he found, to be 1.234m.   He had also noted that 7 ceiling modules were equal to two pillar spacings on the Parthenon flank which, we have seen, varied slightly.   By this latter criterion the ceiling module would have been 1.227m, a difference of only 7mm, so there could have been some minor variation in panel size along the great length.   The dimensions of the modules are close enough to require that the archaeological evidence for the pillar spacing, derived from the stylobate stones of the earlier Parthenon, should no longer be discarded as irrelevant as it seems to have been hitherto.

It can be shown that the ceiling width, as well as the ceiling length, over the peristyles of the earlier Parthenon also fitted the module dimension of the Parthenon ceiling panels in this location.   This would explain the extraordinary and costly measures taken to adjust the inner profile of the peristyle entablature of the Parthenon described in Study 3.   The ceiling panels were already made, complete with the bead and reel detail within the margin around the coffers, cut to suit the ceiling width on the earlier temple   When the width of the peristyle ceiling of the Parthenon became measurable, the architects had to choose between either commissioning a completely new set of ceiling panels, or making the necessary adjustments to the inner face of the peristyle entablature to accommodate the panels already available.   An economic decision was made, based on the availability of human talents, to employ lower grade skills to overcome the problem.

Figure 59 shows the possible arrangement of ceiling beams and panels on the earlier Parthenon compared with that on the Parthenon recorded by Penrose.   From the dimensions of the elements we know about, it is likely that the frieze over the inner porch pillars would have consisted of triglyphs and metopes of the same height as those on the exterior peristyle.   A single step to the naos would have brought all the elements of the entablature into line to support the ceiling beams and panels. The beams across the front peristyle would have been located over the pillars at each end, giving the plan and elevation arrangements shown in figures 60 and 61 leading to the ceiling width shown in figure 62.[7] This is within 4mm of that measured by Penrose on the Parthenon.

(9)   Moulded base stones to the naos wall.

Six blocks of re-used stone, moulded along one edge, were discovered to be built into the western wall of the Parthenon. Only 74mm - the lower half of a torus moulding, had been cut to

---

[7]   Metopes and triglyphs in the frieze over the opisthodomos porch pillars, equal in width as well as height to those on the exterior peristyle at the west end, would have brought about a displacement of the centre of the end porch pillar from its opposite number on the west peristyle of 0.29m.   The beam which spanned the west peristyle located above the end triglyph, is shown the same size as that in the same position on the Parthenon.   This defines the line of the ends of the flank ceiling panels which rest on the wall. Below the cornice course, of which this beam is a part, the frieze course over the naos wall would have been vertical, as it still is on the Parthenon.   The architrave course would have been vertical too, separated from the sloping naos wall face by the anta capital course extended without interruption along the flanks.(see fig.62)   The slope on the wall face would have been at the same degree of inclination as the inner edge of the peristyle pillars, a slope resulting from the combination of 50mm lean and the taper on the pillar.   At pavement level, the opisthodomos porch pillar would have been lined up with the centre line of the surviving anta base stone. This is shown set on the single naos step in the same relationship to it as that later used on the south wall of the Erekhtheion, where the moulded base is identical in height to the earlier Parthenon anta base stone.   This defines a peristyle pavement width of 4.603m.   The other ends of the peristyle ceiling panels are located by a matching projection of the inner cornice course over the inner frieze.   The faces of the frieze and the architrave courses are both vertical and plumb one above the other, the normal arrangement, and these would have been supported by peristyle pillars identical in height and size to those on the Parthenon, but leaning only 50mm in their height. This results in a clear ceiling width of 2.579m, compared to 2.575m on the Parthenon; see figure 62. Figure 63 shows how fine adjustments to both height and span were made on the Parthenon by varying the size and relationship of the interior cornice elements.

Fig. 58 ELEVATIONS OF PILLAR HEAD AND ARCHITRAVE COMPARED

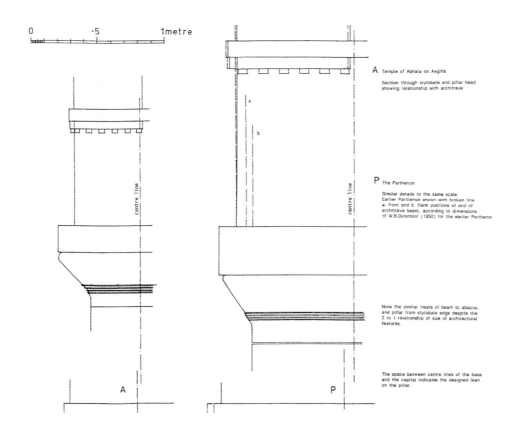

A Temple of Aphaia on Aegina

Section through stylobate and pillar head
showing relationship with architrave

P The Parthenon

Similar details to the same scale.
Earlier Parthenon shown with broken line
a. front and b. flank positions of end of
architrave beam, according to dimensions
of W.B.Dinsmoor (1950) for the earlier Parthenon

Note the similar insets of beam to abacus,
and pillar from stylobate edge despite the
2 to 1 relationship of size of architectural
features.

The space between centre lines of the base
and the capital indicates the designed lean
on the pillar.

Fig. 59 LAYOUT OF CEILING BEAMS AND PANELS COMPARED

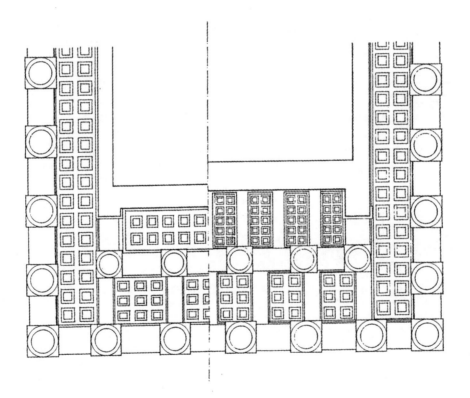

Fig. 60 PLAN OF NORTH WEST CORNER OF THE EARLIER PARTHENON

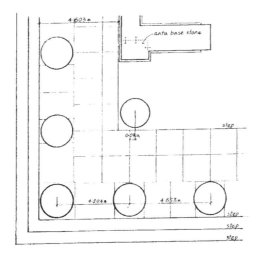

Fig. 61 RELATIONSHIP OF END OPISTHODOMOS PILLAR TO THAT ON THE
WEST FRONT OF THE EARLIER PARTHENON

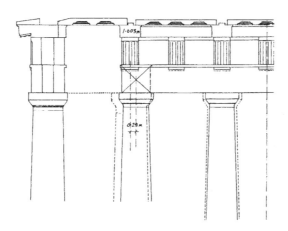

Fig. 62 RELATIONSHIP OF PERISTYLE WIDTH TO CEILING PANEL
ALONG THE FLANK OF THE EARLIER PARTHENON

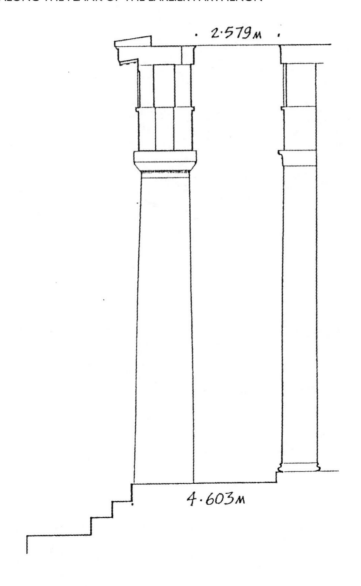

Fig. 63 CROSS SECTIONS THROUGH NORTH PERISTYLE COMPARED

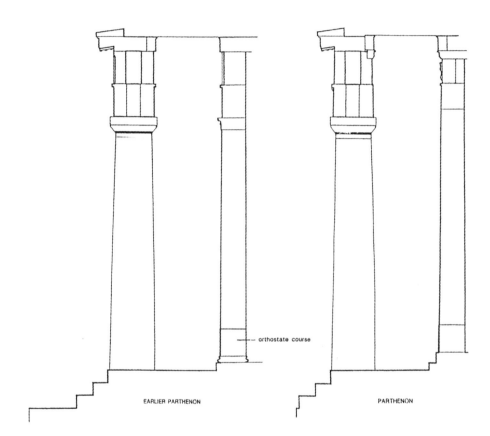

orthostate course

EARLIER PARTHENON

PARTHENON

a finish where its surface would have been inaccessible once the stone was set in its designated position. The total height of the stone was 309mm and it had been originally placed on the naos step to form a projecting base below the lowest, orthostate, course of the naos wall. Because the location was vulnerable during subsequent building operations, the upper part of the stone's exposed edge was left in an S profile, clearly intended to be finished as a full torus below a scotia surmounted by another smaller torus moulding, a pattern which became a 5th century Athenian standard for the bases of Ionic temple pillars and the corresponding walls alongside. Stones of similar profile to those of the earlier Parthenon naos wall base can be seen at the foot of the south wall of the Erekhtheion, where the sequence of mouldings described was elaborated by horizontal fluting of the torus. Penrose recorded that the lower torus on the bases of the Erekhtheion east portico was set 43mm behind the edge of the step on which it sits.

A more complex example of the naos wall base stones was found beneath the pavement of the present Parthenon by agents of Lord Elgin, and was uncovered again in the 1880's by Kavvadias and Kawerau, who failed to recognise what it was. Hill identified it as an anta base stone belonging to the earlier Parthenon. It is a piece of marble measuring slightly over 1.2m x 1.8m and 0.309m thick. It is moulded on two sides but cut on a third in a way which makes clear its function, its probable location and its original longer dimension. It was a base stone to the projecting end of a wall, at the south-east or north-west corner, to be placed upon the step leading into the naos or the opisthodomos. Its shape informed Hill, correctly, that the end one of a series of pillars would have stood in front of it, prostyle. (See figure 60)

Hill supposed that these moulded base stones had survived from the pre-Persian Parthenon because he imagined that, even on a temple of this size, walls and pillars could be built simultaneously.   Study 2 has shown that this was not practical. The number of undoubted pre-Persian elements which remain indicate that only the lower stones from the extreme western end of the earlier temple had been prepared for placing, so it is doubtful if any of the stone for naos elements would have arrived on site by 480 BC. Why?

The working area open for use in the 480's BC. was even less than that available in the 440's, which was very restricted in relation to what was then required. Ross had discovered in the 1830's that charcoal and other debris, which he identified as being from the Persian conflagration of 480 BC., lay 3 - 3.6 metres below the top of the foundation platform, then recently uncovered.   The base of this platform, thought by Dinsmoor to have been started in 488 BC.,[8] lay 5.5 metres below the top of the south-west corner and 12 metres at the south-east, so the plan to raise the ground level here was not only a long-standing one but one already well in hand by 480 BC.   The extent of the platform surface which was left clear around the earlier Parthenon suggests that the ground was still sufficiently below the platform level when the superstructure of that temple was started to require a safe access way all around for scaffolding erectors.   The later Parthenon was able to be sited at the extreme west end of the foundation, indicating perhaps that the ground level there had risen considerably since the Persian occupation.

The presence of the 6th century temple between the building site and the sanctuary of Pandrosos, and the unsuitability of the steeply sloping ground south of the projected temple, an area

---

[8] See Dinsmoor 'The Date of the Older Parthenon' A.J.A.38 1934 pp 418-9.

Fig. 64 VARATIONS IN DIMENSIONS AND RELATIONSHIPS OF STRING
COURSE AND BEAM COURSE ON THE PARTHENON recorded by Penrose

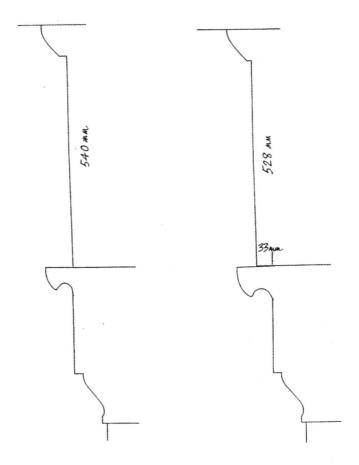

The trimming back of the internal faces of the architrave and frieze courses would have
been done as required, moving from west to east as preparation for lifting into place
the ceiling panels – hence the small variation in the profile and setting of the small and
short lengths of moulded course immediately below.

which was being filled with material brought into the Akropolis sanctuary in order to create a terrace, left a very restricted area open for receiving and working stone delivered from the quarry on Mount Pentelikon.   Stone delivery would have had to be carefully programmed to avoid overcrowding.   More significantly, the anta base stone was found to have three T-shaped cramp cuttings in the top surface, showing it had been placed in position, meaning that the peristyle structure was already in place.   By this token these moulded base stones had to be from a post-Persian-invasion temple built to a pre-Perikleian design.

(10)   Other implications of the anta base stone.

The anta base stone is outlined, dotted, on fig.60 and its dimension on the temple flank face informs us of the unique manner in which the naos wall of the earlier Parthenon was detailed.   On the Parthenon there was a 7mm backward shift of the main wall plane within 0.475m of the anta face.   This was a device used on the Parthenon to provide a termination point for the anta capital on the flank face, a line on which the mouldings of the anta capital could return through 90 degrees into the wall face.   This was done because the architect of that temple wished the sloping face of the wall to continue through the height of the architrave.   Mnesikles repeated the feature throughout the Propylaia wherever he wished to restrict the anta capital to a very narrow strip at the end of a wall.   It gave rise to the architectural form known as a pilaster.   On the earlier Parthenon, it seems there was no such minor change of plane; the mouldings cut on the anta base continued uninterrupted 1.216m along the flank face, with the implication that they continued across the adjacent base stone also.   The anta capital detail too therefore would have continued, as a crown to the inclined section of the naos wall and a line of separation from

Fig. 65 ANTA BASE STONE FROM THE EARLIER PARTHENON

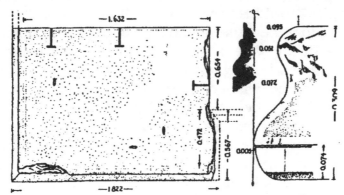

FIGURE 19. — DETAILS OF ANTA BASE OF OLDER PARTHENON.[1]

the vertical face of the architrave above.   The minute set-back to the wall face at the anta, introduced initially on the purely Doric exterior of the Parthenon, was used again, later in the century, on the Ionic temples on the Akropolis, but then with the full complication of the little set-back worked through all the mouldings of the wall base and the anta capital.

(11)   A possible design origin of the anta base stone.

What was the design origin of this Ionic detail, used here at the base of a wall of a Doric temple?   The architect of the earlier Parthenon evidently found no architectural conflict in having it there.   The scale of the other elements nearby was so different; the pillars facing this moulded wall base along the length of the flank peristyle had base diameters over 1.9m and those of the pronaos and opisthodomos ranges, also Doric, over 1.6m, while the height of the moulded base stone was a mere 0.309m.   It seems unlikely, although not impossible, that the pillars within the naos of the earlier Parthenon would have been Ionic, since those of the later Parthenon were Doric, and judging by the close identity of other key elements in the plans for the two temples, major pillars, entablatures and ceiling panels, the pillars inside the naos would most probably have been Doric too.   The only other location where Ionic detail may have been on display would be the treasury.

Where one was incorporated in the plan of a temple, a treasury was bound to be a significant feature and was likely to receive architectural expression in keeping with its special function.   In Athens there were strong connections of language with the other Ionians of the islands and the Asia Minor coast.   It was these, and probably the long-standing and widespread family connections which gave rise to them, which had inspired some Athenians and men from Eretria to go to their aid in 498 BC in

Fig. 66 RECONSTRUCTION OF SECTION ALONG NORTH PERISTYLE OF THE EARLIER
PARTHENON. Temple of Aphaia drawn to the same scale

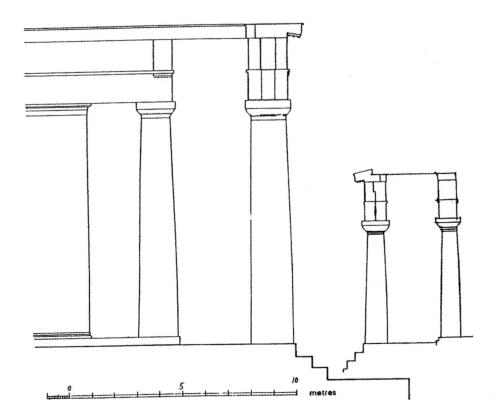

0   5   10   metres

their attempt to free themselves from enemy occupation, an enterprise which resulted in the capture of Sardis from the Persians.
It had been Darius's reprisal for this action in 490 which had
ended in the amazing Athenian victory at Marathon, and it was
to celebrate the victory that a new temple was being planned in
the early 480's.   So it is not surprising that Athene's treasury
should be included in the temple plan; nor would it be a surprise
to find the softer, more lyrical forms of the Ionic style of
architecture employed in the internal design of the treasury.
Here again the remaining evidence is slight.   There are pieces of
the unfinished profile of a moulded base stone, 0.309m high,
some of which could have come from the internal foot of the
treasury wall, and there are the recorded marks on the floor of
the later Parthenon showing that the roof over the widened
treasury in that temple was carried on only four pillars, whose
base diameter where they rested on the floor was 1.786m.

Fortunately there is also a full Ionic order displaying great
maturity of design and erected in the mid 430's, within a few
years of the completion of the Parthenon, which still exists in the
interior of the Propylaia.   This was carefully noted by Penrose,
and it is the strange design of the base of these pillars which
gives a clue to what the Ionic order used in the Parthenon
treasury would have been like. The unusual feature of the
Propylaia pillar base is the flared profile introduced beneath the
sequence of torus-scotia-torus which became the characteristic
organisation for Ionic pillar bases throughout the rest of the 5th
century examples in Athens.   There seems to be no reason for
the insertion of the flared profile below the base mouldings in the
Ionic order of the Propylaia, where the pavement upon which the
six pillars stood was level. However, this was not the case in the
Parthenon treasury where, as fig.9 has shown, there were
complex slopes on the floor towards the perimeter walls to the
west, north and south from the highest datum point in the

Fig. 67 SUGGESTED SECTIONS THROUGH THE TREASURIES

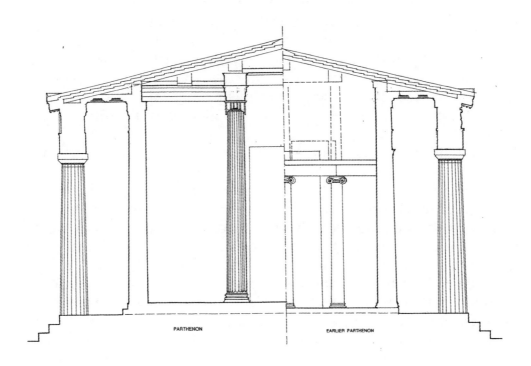

PARTHENON   EARLIER PARTHENON

Fig. 68 IONIC BASE ON PROPYLAIA, flare worked on pavement stones.

Fig. 69 PENROSE'S PLATE 32

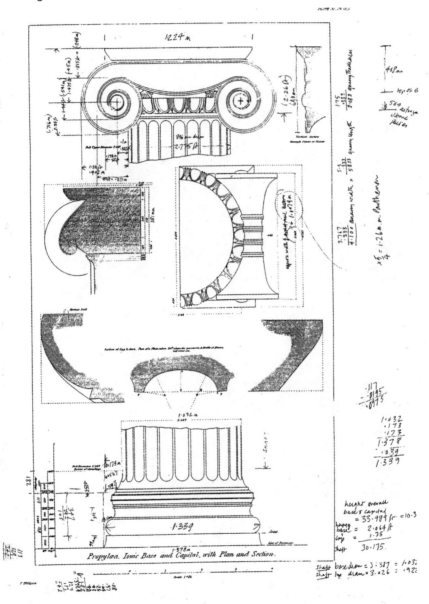

centre of the east wall.   In addition, the four pillars in the treasury would have needed to lean slightly towards the centre line of the room in order to support the line of major roof beams which are indicated by recesses in the cross walls.   These were measured and drawn by Penrose on his plate 16.(see fig.37)   A centre line for the pillars, connecting the base marks on the floor and the beam recesses in the cross wall, would be inclined in a similar way to the sloping jambs of the doorway.   Any Ionic pillar used in the Parthenon treasury would have needed another element below the lowest torus to take up the complex slopes of where the leaning pillar met the floor sloping in two opposite directions.   Had it sat directly on the floor, the lower torus moulding would have been either distorted or partially eaten away by such slopes.   A flared profile would have coped with this problem more sensitively than any other form, without the slopes being detectable by the human eye, and this is the most likely explanation for the origin and use of an unusual flared base worked on to the floor panel under the pillar.

The inference is that when Mnesikles - undoubtedly trained on the Parthenon, talented, but judging from some minor aberrations revealed at roof level on the gatehouse, still quite young - was asked to design the Propylaia he was faced with enough difficulties.   It was a complex planning problem on a fearsomely sloping site, requiring speedy resolution and realisation.   Rather than setting out to invent a completely new Ionic order of architecture to suit his needs within the gatehouse, he would have borrowed a design already in existence in the Parthenon. In the circumstances it would be understandable that he should carry through the flared element along with the rest, only reducing its relative height in proportion to the rest of the order. Excluding the flare in each case, there would have been a simple 5:4 dimensional relationship between the Ionic pillar in the Parthenon treasury and that in the Propylaia.   In the Parthenon this would result in a total pillar height of 13m including a flared base fitting the diameter detected on the floor of the Parthenon. As Penrose's plate 16 shows, this pillar would have reached the top of the naos walls, upon which would have rested the architrave beams supporting the ceiling and roof timbers. The spans of the architraves inside the treasury were probably too long to have been of stone, particularly as the depth of them, if those in the Propylaia were made proportional to them, would have resulted in their being smaller than those over the peristyle pillars. They could have been assembled using long sections of pine, one above another, keyed together with oak inserts, those used vertically being set at raking angles to inhibit deflection, and the three-fascia profile designed to mask the horizontal joints between the layers of timber in the composite beam.

Fig.67 shows the suggested sections through the treasuries of the earlier and the later Parthenon alongside one another; note the introduction on the Parthenon of a second step to the naos, the lower of which happens to be the same height as the abandoned moulded base stone at the foot of the earlier wall, perhaps an attempt to keep the overall wall height of the Parthenon equal to that of its predecessor and thereby in line with the top of the peristyle entablature. The height of the moulded base of the Ionic pillar shown here, one which, it is suggested, would have been the model used by Mnesikles, reduced in the ratio 5:4 in the Propylaia, relates to the moulded base stones of the earlier Parthenon in the exact ratio 3:2. This suggests that the moulded anta base was also the pattern and size of pillar bases inside the treasury of the earlier Parthenon and thus the original of the design copied and altered only in scale by, in turn, the architect of the Parthenon and the architect of the Propylaia. It would have been an architectural arrangement employed for the first time here, but one exploited many times later, on the Temple of Artemis Agrotera on the Ilissos, the

Fig. 70 IONIC BASE PROFILES ON THE ATHENIAN AKROPOLIS

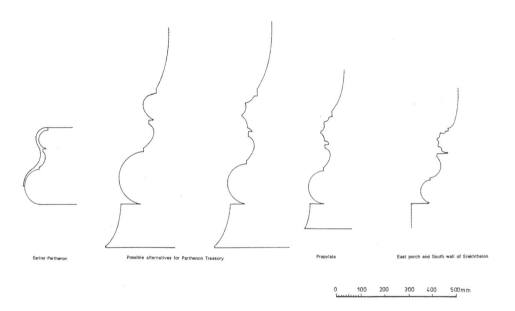

Earlier Parthenon   Possible alternatives for Parthenon Treasury   Propylaia   East porch and South wall of Erekhtheion

0   100   200   300   400   500mm

Nike temple on the bastion at the entrance to the Akropolis and on the Erekhtheion east porch and south wall, where the height of the moulded section is the same as that of the surviving anta base stone of the earlier Parthenon. With this size of pillar in the treasury, the earlier Parthenon would have had a gallery with a superimposed order above to support the ceiling.   The pillars would have been set out at about 2.775m centres in the east-west direction, like those in the naos and aligned with them. They could have carried plain architrave beams, like those later used on the temple on the Ilissos, here in the treasury spanning in the north-south direction and 3.4m long, with a central row of pillars at ground level only, to support the timber floor of the gallery.   The capitals were then so aligned that whoever entered was faced by their fourteen pairs of intimidating owl-like eyes, probably gilded to reflect the light from the opened doorway.

Figure 70 shows, to a common scale, the moulded anta base stone of the earlier Parthenon, with an outline of how it would have been finished; two alternative base profiles, either of which may have been used in the Parthenon, one a straight enlargement of what was inherited from the earlier temple with the addition of the necessary flare, the other the Parthenon architect's possible redesign of the whole base moulding sequence to accommodate the flare; the base of the pillar from the Propylaia, and that of the east porch and south wall of the Erekhtheion.   The following table shows the detailed dimensions of the Ionic pillars in the earlier Parthenon and the Parthenon if they were related to those in the Propylaia in the way suggested. It may be that hitherto unidentified fragments bear some similarities to them, or that these pillar shafts of the earlier and later temples were re-used elsewhere.

	EARLIER PARTHENON	PARTHENON	PROPYLAIA
Height of moulded base	0.309m	0.463m	0.372m
Height of flared base below	N/A	0.174m	0.099m
Height of pillar without flare	8.550m	12.825m	10.260m
Height of architrave beam	0.697m	1.046m	0.837m
Diameter of flared base	N/A	1.786m	1.378m
Diameter over lower torus	1.116m	1.674m	1.339m
Lower shaft diameter	0.860m	1.290m	1.032m
Upper shaft diameter	0.705m	1.057m	0.846m
Length of capital overall	1.375m	2.062m	1.650m
Width of capital at abacus	0.957m	1.435m	1.026m
Length of abacus	1.020m	1.530m	1.224m
Centres of eyes	0.855m	1.282m	1.026m

|_____2:3_____|
                        |_____5:4_____|
|_____5:6_____|

Later, with the figure of Athene clothed in gold proposed by Pheidias for the Parthenon, a substantial part of her treasure would have been accommodated in the naos.   This, and the fact that the treasury, like the naos, was to be increased in width, meant that the need for a gallery would not be so great.   The treasury would then become subject to another of Pheidias's grandiose ideas, and the Ionic pillars could be enlarged in the 3:2 ratio applied elsewhere in the transition from one Parthenon design to another, enabling the pillars to soar to the upper ceiling level.

This description of the treasuries in both the earlier and the later Parthenon is hypothetical.   It is based on a close observation and analysis of all the detail which remained for Penrose to record in 1846-7.   The detail exhibits simple mathematical relationships which are not only precise but also deliver unsuspected yet logical links between pillar base profiles, their diameters and the heights of the rooms they occupied.

(12)   A reconstructed plan of the earlier Parthenon compared with the later.

Figure 71 shows a plan of the earlier Parthenon reconstructed from the archaeological evidence described above, super-imposed on the plan of the later Parthenon.   As one would expect in a supreme work of art, there was little in the designed fabric of either Parthenon which was superfluous.   Every minute feature told a story; sometimes, in the case of the later temple, a secret story of its history, but most often the feature proclaimed its design purpose.   Nothing was left to chance.   That was why precision of execution was always of paramount importance. While much of the material in the Periklean building was re-used from an earlier version, that re-cycling was not advertised.   It was hidden from view, disguised in favour of changes which would improve on the original, where that was possible, by increased liveliness of line, greater tautness in the solid:void ratios of the major elements, but most of all by a change in the balance of the relationship of the architecture with the sculpture. It was through simple numerical relationships that designs were transposed from one scale to another and perpetuated.   It was through exquisite refinement that the tradition of Athenian architecture developed throughout the 5th century.   The other major factor in the continuity of this tradition which can be observed was one which some scholars have been unwilling to acknowledge, a human one – the architects and designers who were involved in the process.   This will be explored in the study which follows.

Fig. 71 TEMPLES OF ATHENE. Plans of Parthenon and Earlier Parthenon superimposed

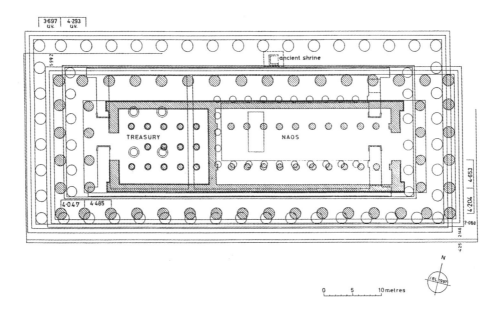

Fig. 72 PARTHENON EAST FRONTS COMPARED

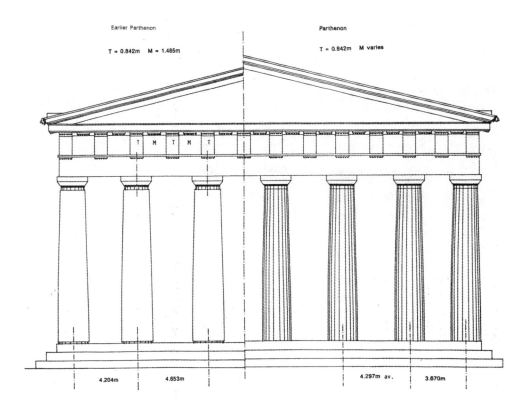

Earlier Parthenon

T = 0.842m   M = 1.485m

Parthenon

T = 0.842m   M varies

4.204m   4.653m   4.297m av.   3.670m

5   THE ARCHITECTS

Who were the architects of the Parthenon, this temple which was built twice?   No written record has been traced of the building of the earlier Parthenon, yet it has been known since the mid-nineteenth century that parts of the earliest manifestation of its design - the temple which was barely started before it was almost completely destroyed by the Persians in 480 BC - still exist immured in the north wall of the Athenian Akropolis.   So contemporary epigraphic records, valuable as they are where they exist, cannot be seriously considered to hold a monopoly of authority on the history of Athenian architecture in the 5th century BC.   Other marks on stone, made by structural masons rather than letter cutters, can be reliable sources of testimony.

(1)   Possible candidates for authorship of the earlier Parthenon

Not all the stones damaged in 480 BC. were used to strengthen the north wall.   Some were deliberately left in place in order to facilitate what the architects knew to be the trickiest stage of the re-building of the temple, the setting out of the stylobate to its upwardly curved form.   That work could be resumed only after the more urgent matters of restoring the houses and the civic offices of the shattered city had been completed.   Nevertheless, someone was present on the Akropolis in 479 who knew the difference between the stones which were expendable and the time-saving value of what was better left in place.   Much of the fire-damaged stonework in the stylobate and the step below, as well as the pillar bases, were removed to strengthen the north wall of the Akropolis towards the easterly end (see fig.1).   The lowest step, equally badly damaged by fire, was left as a helpful guide to repeating the subtle curve which had been painstakingly worked on it.   This would be useful when work on the temple could be resumed, so it was left in place even though it would have to be covered up by moving the replacement steps to the south and west by a step width.   This, and what came after, suggests that this person was the architect of the temple, who had survived those traumatic years.   The skilled way in which the sections of entablature, rescued from the collapsed structure of the Athene Polias temple, were built into the more westerly part of the north wall (see fig.2), facing the city as a memorial of what had been lost, reveals that the work was managed by someone who understood the past context of what was being preserved.   This was in sharp contrast to the way in which the discarded stones were assembled to construct the projecting corners of the same range of wall further to the east in a hurried attempt to strengthen the northerly defences, at the instigation of Themistokles.[1]   In a similarly careful fashion, the surviving pediment sculptures from the ancient temples, some of which had been taken down by the Athenians ten years earlier from the dismantled Hekatompedon and presumably set up on display within the Akropolis, since that is where they were found with others defaced by the marauding Persians in 480/79, were all buried on the site along with the many votive sculptures from the 6th century which had been similarly abused.   They were to remain unseen until the excavation of 1886.   When Penrose saw them soon after they were uncovered, he was struck by the similarity of some of the female sculptures to the figures taken from the Temple of Aphaia in 1811, which he had seen in Munich.   *"They seemed to have suffered, in the first instance, from intentional violence, but had been afterwards laid down where they were found, and some of them were covered with slabs of stone. ....some....were found in a small chamber".*[2]   If, as has been implied in study 4, the architect of the earlier Parthenon had connections with Aigina, then the sculptor could

[1] See Thucydides 1. 93
[2] Penrose 2nd. edition p.5

186

have been known to him and this, added to the natural reverence for votive objects which had been the victims of sacrilege, could have inspired the act of preservation.

Identifying the architect of the earlier Parthenon by name can only be conjecture, although what has been discovered about the building tells us a great deal about him as an artist.   The preceding studies have shown the likelihood that most of the stones from the building activity which resumed on the site in the 460's have survived as parts of the Parthenon.   Anyone who was capable of defining profiles of such serene yet stirring quality, having so subtle a freedom of line combined with a tautness which makes them sing, who was bold enough to incorporate them in a building conceived on a massive scale, capable of devising the techniques of having them realised in Pentelic marble, when there was no-one around with the experience to advise him, and who was dogged enough to oversee the work being carried out faithfully to his vision over a period of thirty years, must have been an extraordinary man.   It may be thought that his name is irrelevant; an ancient Greek would not have thought so, and to ignore any clues which might reveal it to us would be a denial of natural justice to such a man.

In the public record of the building accounts of the later Parthenon, the names of two architects are associated with the project which was initiated by Perikles and started in 447 BC, Iktinos and Kallikrates, and Plutarch repeated this attribution in his life of Perikles.[3]   It is the other references to these two names which might indicate which, if either of them, could have been the architect of the earlier Parthenon.

---

[3] Plutarch 'Perikles' 13.

Fig. 73 PROFILES OF MOULDINGS USED ON THE PARTHENON

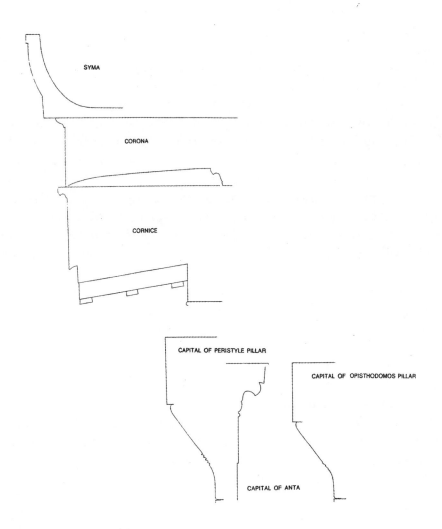

It has been mentioned that Vitruvius referred in his 'De Architectura' to a book about the Parthenon written by Iktinos and someone called Karpion.   There is no other surviving reference to Karpion, but Iktinos was mentioned by Pausanias as the architect of a temple to Apollo at Bassai in Arkadia, and his plan to enlarge the Hall of the Mysteries at Eleusis in the 430's has come down to us, cut into the rock foundation. Although the dates of these structures are not certain, they are both late enough to rule out Iktinos as having been the designer of the earlier Parthenon started in the 480's.

(2)   The case for Kallikrates as architect of the earlier Parthenon.

The other references to Kallikrates appear to pose a strange contradiction to his being named in the 447/6 building accounts as one of two architects of the Parthenon.   His appointment to this, the most prestigious project of all Perikles's building enterprises, which could be expected to occupy many years of a man's life, might be thought to preclude involvement in much other work, judging from the pace at which the work proceeded. Yet Kallikrates was also appointed, at about the same time, to carry out one other major work, the building of the Middle Long Wall between Athens and Peiraieus, and two other smaller commissions.   These are referred to in inscriptions IG I³ 35 and IG I³ 45.

I. S. Mark[4] dated the inscription IG I³ 35 to the mid-5th century on the basis of its letter forms and what he called *"the attested career of Kallikrates"*.   This, the Nike temple decree, called for Kallikrates to fit the sanctuary with doors, and provide the specifications for the building of a small naos or temple, and an

---

[4] Mark 'Athena Nike' Hesperia Supplement 1993.

altar of worked stone.   The inscription was discovered in 1897.
The dismembered blocks of a small amphiprostyle temple had
been collected together and rebuilt on the Nike bastion in the
1830's by Ross, Schaubert and Hansen.   Kavvadias dated the
inscription at around 450 BC and thought this temple was from
the same date.   Later, in 1893, Fürtwangler considered 426 as a
more likely date for the temple.   In 1910 A.A. Korte proposed
that while the decree related to the temple rebuilt by Ross and
others, there had been a delay of 25 years in implementing it
caused, he suggested, by the political conflict between Perikles
and his conservative opponents.[5]   The effect of this was to link
Kallikrates's name with the amphiprostyle temple now standing
on the Nike bastion, and by doing so extended his supposed
career across the third quarter of the century.   In 1916
F.Studniczka linked the little temple on the river Ilissos, which
had been measured by Stuart and Revett before its destruction
by the Turks in 1778, with the Nike temple which it resembled
closely, and Kallikrates's name was then associated with that
temple too.

W.B. Dinsmoor subscribed to this line of scholarship concerning
the Nike temple.   He also linked the Hephaisteion, the Temple of
Ares, the Temple of Poseidon at Sounion and the Temple of
Nemesis at Rhamnous together as works carried out under the
same hand of what he called an *"un-named Theseum architect"*.

Mrs I.M. Shear[6] developed the observations of earlier scholars
from Puchstein (1887) onwards, into a case for identifying
Kallikrates as the designer of the Athene Nike temple, the temple
on the Ilissos, the temple of the Athenians on the island of Delos
and even the Erekhtheion, which was completed as late as

---

[5] The source of the story used by Rhys Carpenter to suggest Kallikrates and Iktinos
were rivals, an idea at variance with their joint appointment.
[6] Shear 'Kallikrates' Hesperia 1963.

405 BC. The reasoning appeared sound enough. There are undeniable similarities between the various buildings; in their plan arrangement, the sequence of their mouldings, the shapes of the mouldings themselves, the detailed form of their Ionic capitals, and the inclination or lack of it of elements of their structure. However, on the same basis, there are similarities between the Propylaia and the Erekhtheion which need to be otherwise explained before the logic of these arguments can be made complete, since we were told by Plutarch that Mnesikles designed the Propylaia.[7]

Rhys Carpenter[8] took the definition of a supposed professional career of Kallikrates further, attributing to him all the Doric buildings which Dinsmoor had attributed, by similar characteristics of style, to the *"un-named Theseum architect"*, although he was content to *"leave aside"* the possibility of Kallikrates's connection with the Erekhtheion. Presumably this was because he wished to extend Kallikrates's working life back to 465 BC., having him design what he called a *"Kimonian"* Parthenon, built in the 460's. Being committed to the promotion of Kallikrates as the *"Theseum"* architect, Carpenter was loth to think too publicly about who the designer of the pre-Persian-invasion Parthenon could have been, despite his acknowledgement that there was no discernable difference between the design of this earliest Parthenon and what he called the *"Kimonian"* temple which he said was by Kallikrates. J.A. Bundgaard, who had also postulated a *"Kimonian"* Parthenon designed by Kallikrates, simply denied there had ever been a pre-Persian Parthenon.

---

[7] Plutarch 'Perikles' 13.
[8] Carpenter 'The Architects of the Parthenon' 1970.

In 1936 N. Balanos had been asked to strengthen the walls of the Nike bastion and he discovered, some two metres beneath the temple, remains of a small earlier naos and altar. Bundgaard drew attention to the close correspondence between the Nike temple decree and the remains which Balanos had uncovered.[9] I.S. Mark's subsequent exposition of the history of the Athene Nike temple finally severed the connection of Kallikrates with the Athene Nike temple which we can see today, making it clear that his commission was for the smaller and earlier phase of the development of the sanctuary, limited to those works which underlie the present temple.

The reputation of the innocent Kallikrates has seemed to suffer at the hands of I.S. Mark as a consequence of this discovery, since he went on to write *"Kallikrates may well have been in charge of several Akropolis projects of relatively unassuming nature"*[10]. IG I^3 45 perhaps, but the Parthenon too?

The inscription IG I^3 45 confirms Kallikrates's appointment to carry out repairs to the north wall of the Akropolis, but rather than that being a reflection on his lowly status, contradicted by his appointment as one of two architects to rebuild the Parthenon, there could be quite another logic connecting all four appointments.

Firstly, the north wall repairs. If it was Kallikrates who had been the architect of the earlier Parthenon, and therefore the most likely man to have arranged the careful repair of the suspected breach at the west end of the north wall, and seen to the building-in of the rescued entablatures in 479 BC., he would have been the obvious choice for the repair work and the

---

[9] Bundgaard 'Le sujet de IG1· 24' Melanges Helleniques offerts a George Daux., Paris 1974.
[10] Mark 'Athena Nike' p.132.

building of the parapet in 449.   This was carried out with stone from Aigina, as was the little naos for Athene Nike.   Aigina was, by the early 440's, paying tribute to Athens and the supply of stone could have been considered part payment in kind.   The architect of the earlier Parthenon would have been familiar with the quarry and its product.

Secondly, the Nike naos and sanctuary.   This was a commission which was minor in scale, but sensitive in both its religious and political aspects.   Mark has suggested that the priesthood set up by the same decree was probably new.[11]   If that were so, who would be better to give advice at those early stages than a man who had been the trusted advisor to the priesthood of Athene since the time of Marathon, if he were still alive?   If longer term plans were being already thought about for the westerly approach to the Akropolis, then sensible though modest interim arrangements were vital to the nurturing of the cult.   If the cult was of long standing, then the political advantages to Perikles of employing the earlier Parthenon architect would be even more relevant.

Thirdly, the Middle Long Wall.   Two earlier walls, one to the north-west and the other to the south-east, connected the city with the port and, since Athens was some 4 miles from the sea, a substantial area of land was enclosed between them.   Peiraieus had been an island, cut off from the mainland by the marshes of Halipedon, and it was probably Themistokles's vision of Peiraieus as a port which led to the two defensive walls being built to secure Athens' sea-borne life lines, starting with the wall to the north-west.   They were completed around 456 BC.   It seems that for several years Perikles had wanted a third wall, within arrow range of that facing towards Megara, and he finally won

---

[11] Mark 'Athena Nike' p.104-107 and n.61.

193

approval for the project around the mid-century. The completion of this wall is recorded in the Athenian building accounts of the year V 443/2 BC. In terms of scope and cost the building of the Middle Long Wall was a major undertaking which required experience in dealing with the serious foundation problems which had been encountered in building the first walls where they crossed the swampy ground near Peiraieus.[12] The choice of Kallikrates for this work and the timing of it is of more significance than has been recognised hitherto, since it suggests that, far from being an architect suitable for appointment to oversee only minor works, he already had this kind of experience.   He could have acquired this knowledge only if he had been involved in similar projects in the past.   All of these, the building of the first two Long Walls and the south and east perimeter walls of the Akropolis, the latter carried out necessarily for the resumption of work on the earlier Parthenon, had been commissioned during the time of Kimon's ascendancy.   The supervision of such projects was not onerous.   Once a pattern of procedure was established and reliable master masons were selected to see to the day to day running of the contracts for the various stretches of the wall, the highly repetitive work could easily be overseen by the appointed architect's assistants.   Only when unusual problems arose, such as foundation difficulties, would specialised knowledge or ingenuity need to come into play. His long experience of setting up and managing building contracts of all kinds would have made the architect of the earlier Parthenon, if he were still alive, the natural choice as contractor for the Middle Wall.

Fourthly, the Parthenon.   If a young man had been appointed to be the architect of the earlier Parthenon, he would have been at least thirty years of age in 489 and seventy in 449 BC., old and

---

[12] Plutarch 'Kimon' 13.

probably unwilling to start, yet again, on the rebuilding of his temple.   But, quite apart from the political advantage of having him officially connected with the enterprise, to take some of the wind from the sails of those who would be violently opposed to taking down a temple which they and their fathers had helped to finance, he would have been a valuable appointee to advise on how to dismantle the nearly completed temple, since he had designed in great detail the method of putting it together. Experienced in all the techniques required, he would also have understood the logistics of site organisation necessary for such an intricate procedure, which involved knowing where to dispose the dismembered parts in the most efficient order, so that they could be readily re-used.   By no means least in importance, he would have had personal acquaintance with the masons he could rely on to supervise the taking down of the temple and who Iktinos would have to rely on to carry out the rebuilding.

The architect of the earlier Parthenon had already dismantled the old Hekatompedon to clear a site for his own temple project, storing the parts carefully so that they could be re-used, as later they were, some of the metopes outside the entrance to the Akropolis, many of the stones at the lower levels of Kimon's great south wall.   The idea of taking the earlier Parthenon apart in order to enlarge it for Pheidias's Athene Parthenos statue would not have appeared so daunting as it might seem to us today.   It should not be forgotten that the Parthenon itself, or what remained of it, was reconstructed twice in the last 75 years of the 20th.century, in efforts to conserve it and prolong its life.

(3)   Evidence of a school of design in Athens in the 5th century BC.

What, then, is the explanation of the similarities so acutely observed by so many scholars, within both the group of Athenian

Doric temples and the Ionic temples also?   It is not only on the major buildings of the 5th century that such common characteristics of detail have been found.   L.S. Merritt[13] has noted that some of the features of the Painted Stoa in the Agora, such as the wall crown moulding, are similar to details in the work of the *"un-named Theseum"* architect.   She noted too that the masonry of the steps found in the Propylon, a forerunner of the present Propylaia, exhibited the same meticulous care found in the pedestal of the Athene Promakhos statue and the upper, dressed courses of the Parthenon platform, similarities also noted by Dinsmoor[14]   and Bundgaard.[15]

It is important to remember that in a culture of tradition, which the practice of architecture was in the ancient Greek world, the giving or handing on, both of what has long been known and what has just been learned, is the essential process for continuity and gradual development.   Inherited artifacts such as tools, patterns, profiles, drawings. have always been necessary ingredients in the making of tradition.   It is to be expected that features of architectural design, working through patterns and profiles of mouldings, would be handed on to aspiring younger architects, men themselves well grounded in masonry skills and showing, in addition, organisational talents which could be developed by a good teacher.   It is surely through such a process of schooling that a design dynasty, strong enough to persist in recognisable form in Athens throughout the 5th century, could give rise to the perception of Dinsmoor and others of certain unifying characteristics of style, to the authorship of which names could not be securely attached in the absence of historical documentation.   Dinsmoor's dating of the various temples which he attributed to a person he called the *"Theseum"* architect,

---

[13] Merritt 'Stoa Poikile, Athens' Hesperia 39 1970.
[14] Dinsmoor 'A.A.G.'1950.
[15] Bundgaard 'Mnesicles' 1957.

placed them in a chronological sequence, first of all because he assumed that only one person was responsible for them, and also that he seems to have believed that Athenian architects worked alone and could not be engaged in more than one project at a time, three fallacies which should not be allowed to discolour the questions of either the authorship or the dates of 5th century buildings.   M.M.Miles has already breached these dams to progress in these fields.[16]

Dinsmoor did not consider the more likely alternative, that at least one many-handed architectural practice, or a co-operative, was involved in the work, a system boosted by Perikles's ambitious building programme set in motion in 448BC.   Like all human enterprises, these groups of practitioners included men with unequal gifts; some, like the nameless authors of the Hephaisteion, competent but without that spark of inspiration which can lift a building on to another level of communication, a plane inhabited by the Parthenon, which seems always to have impressed its viewers through its purely plastic presence.   There can be little doubt that the group of architects trained by the designer of the earlier Parthenon, who must have been pre-eminent among his fellows, were profoundly influenced by him, most of all by the high standards of accuracy and skill he was able to persuade them to require of their workmen.   The circumstantial evidence outlined above persuades me that his name was Kallikrates.

Without doubt, as architect of the earlier Parthenon, he was the most innovative of all the architects working in Athens during the 5th century.   He launched enough themes and ideas in one building to sustain his colleagues throughout the rest of the

---

[16] Miles 'A Reconstruction of the Temple of Nemesis at Rhamnous' Hesperia 58 1989 p.222.

century.   Mnesikles relied heavily on the precedents set by him, as did the architect of the Erekhtheion, the latter adding the elaboration - some would say over-elaboration - of the decoration applied to the Ionic bases and the capitals of the pillars, and the brilliant use of caryatids to support the roof of the south porch.

(4)   The role of Iktinos.

What of Iktinos?   It would seem that he contributed little in the way of new detailed forms in his reconstruction of the temple. The flared base to the Ionic pillars in the treasury of the Parthenon is one of only two new elements he brought to the design. This had its own progenitive qualities, being copied by Mnesikles on a smaller scale and in a more restrained manner in the Propylaia.   While he evidently liked the appearance of the flare, Mnesikles does not seem to have understood its function as Iktinos did.   The Ionic interior at Bassai, attributed to Iktinos on the reporting of Pausanias, is the work of a man who had developed an enthusiasm for the flared base, producing an exaggerated form of it in the Temple of Apollo which verges on the bizarre.   The designer flared even the flutes outward to a small torus moulding, and below this extended the width of the base greatly with a large flare sitting above another, smaller one.

In Athens the 'flaring tendency' manifested itself in the pillar bases on two small temples, that on the Ilissos and that of Nike Apteros at the entrance to the Akropolis, in the form of an increase in height of the ovolo moulding, relative to the torus mouldings above and below. This was further exaggerated on the Nike example by a reduction of the height of the lower torus, which had the effect of making the ovolo the major element, looking more like a flare. The design of the bases to the pillars of the Erekhtheion porches show a return to the unaffected original used on the earlier Parthenon, with the ovolo kept in balanced

Fig. 74 IONIC BASE USED AT BASSAI

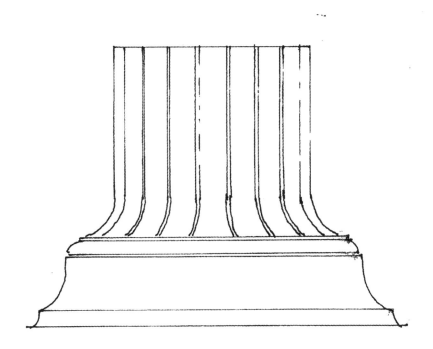

Fig 75 IONIC BASE PROFILES

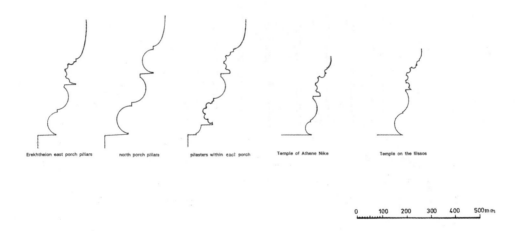

Erekhtheion east porch pillars   north porch pillars   pilasters within east porch   Temple of Athene Nike   Temple on the Ilissos

0   100   200   300   400   500mm

proportion to the height of the torus mouldings, but extended outwards just enough to achieve, on the north porch, a profile which suggests perfect stability. A minuscule flare was reproduced at the bottom of the base of the anta pilasters on the south wall behind the east porch, a last flicker of this fashion as it died out with the end of the century.

The other feature contributed by Iktinos to the design of the Parthenon was the way of arresting the anta capital moulding, by the device of breaking the plane of the wall, of which it is the end part, and creating the effect of a slightly projecting pilaster. This too became a feature beloved by Mnesikles, who used it throughout the Propylaia to articulate the end of a stretch of wall. It is one of those features which would persuade some scholars that Mnesikles could have been the architect of the Nike temple and of the Erekhtheion, because it is used on both. On the latter it is used systematically, although with great reserve on the Ionic walls, in order to manage the conflicts of form arising from the collision of disparate elements of which the temple is composed. This can be seen particularly at the west end. It is a feature from Aphaia which was not used on the earlier Parthenon, as the surviving anta base stone testifies; there were no little shifts of plane interrupting the flow of surface and line intended for the naos walls of that temple. Iktinos replaced the dynamic idea of the wall design on the earlier Parthenon with a concept of lightly articulated order in the Parthenon, still to be found in the Temple of Aphaia on Aigina, rejected by Kallikrates, it was resurrected by Iktinos. It is a curious irony that the schema of the naos walls of the earlier Parthenon would have been much more in tune with the free-flowing frieze introduced by Pheidias than the context produced for it by Iktinos, who lacked the Attic eye.

Apart from those details which he discarded, like the Ionic wall base, Iktinos was content to copy the details which had been there before. His spacing arrangements of ceiling beams over the east and west peristyles and over the pronaos and opisthodomos lobbies are regular but off-beat from the rhythm of the pillars.[17] The panels which they supported over the west peristyle were composed, not of square coffers, like those along the north and south sides, but ones made slightly off square, no doubt to accommodate the resulting dimensions of the voids the panels were to fill. The ribs between the coffers were similar in width to those used along the north and south peristyles. These may have been features of the panels used here on the earlier Parthenon too; figure 59 shows the form the ceiling panels would then have taken, although this is governed by the width given to the west peristyle pavement in the reconstruction of the plan (fig.57) for which dimension there is no firm evidence. Neither is there clear evidence for the depth of the opisthodomos lobby shown in this reconstruction of the earlier Parthenon, although, as drawn, the resulting ceiling panels over it could have had square coffers separated by ribs of the same width as those over the peristyle, but without the bead and reel moulding being used. The smaller coffers used over the lobby to the opisthodomos of the Parthenon are simply a repeated version of the peristyle coffer design scaled down to fit unusually long and narrow inter-beam spaces.

The evidence points to Iktinos not being a product of any Athenian school. The manner in which the foundation platform was extended to the north is out of character with Athenian practice. Even though the bulk of the podium built by the architect of the earlier Parthenon was to be buried beneath the planned terrace, the whole structure consisted of regular courses

---

[17] Penrose plate 15.

Fig. 76 EXTENSION OF PARTHENON FOUNDATIONS AT NORTH-WEST CORNER

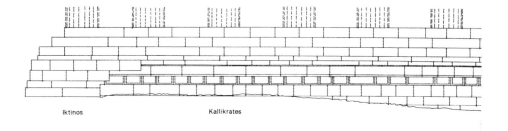

Iktinos   Kallikrates

bonded one to another by the stones in alternate levels being laid at right angles to those above and below. In the extension, regular coursing was abandoned. This may have been a deliberate act to ensure that the ground level all around the temple had to be raised further, even though it meant covering up also several courses of the carefully faced stonework of the earlier Parthenon podium.

When he came to lay down the stylobate of the Parthenon to new lines of upward curvature, Iktinos rejected the stylobate stones of the earlier Parthenon and obtained from the quarry a completely new set of these costly items in order to set out his version of the temple to the new dimensions of his plan. He centred the pillars on the joints between two stones instead of the base drums straddling three, as they had on the older temple (see fig.51). There may have been sound, if obscure, reasons for doing this, connected with the varied slopes given to the bottom of the base stones being rendered incorrect by the increased upward curvature given to the stylobate, but this could scarcely have been too much to be accommodated in a reworking of the contact surfaces, and the impression given to the observant, and in some cases hostile, laymen would have been one of profligacy - not an Athenian trait in the 5th century B.C.

The mystifying appearance of regulae and guttae at the top of the architrave beams resting on the pronaos pillars, and the corresponding ones at the west end, where a continuously carved frieze surmounts both, rendering the detail pointless and superfluous, may suggest that there was a last minute change of plan, to substitute a carved frieze for one with alternating triglyphs and metopes which was originally intended. This decision would have had to be made during stage two of the erection process at the latest, as stage three included the placing of the frieze stones at the west end. (See figs. 27 and 28) The design of such a fully figured frieze, the ordering of material from the quarry and the building in of the stones for its execution would have caused serious delay if it had been thought of only when the architrave stones had been set up, and we know that the temple was built speedily.   Moreover, it would have been known by the time the opisthodomos pillars were erected, that the overall height of the entablature above them had to be revised in order to line up the cornice course with that of the peristyle entablature opposite.   The opisthodomos architrave height was then drastically reduced by 304mm in the attempt to do this, but it was not enough to achieve a level ceiling.   The 54mm displacement revealed by Penrose's measured section here, (plate 16 see fig. 37) could have been taken up in the height of the frieze stones being ordered from the quarry.   The fact that it was not suggests that the new design of at least the west frieze was already fully worked out to a height which would result in a misalignment at ceiling level, with the implication that the method of resolving the problem had also been already determined in order to avoid affecting the height of the frieze. The masons making architrave beams to sit over Doric pillars already erected, would automatically carve on them half regulae at the ends and a full regula at the centre.   But who instructed them about their size here?   And why were they not told to cut them away to make the architrave course continuous as it was on the flanks, where it corresponds better with the free forms in the frieze above?

Iktinos may have lacked the experience to control practical building processes, but he was resourceful in resolving the conflicts which ensued.   He was highly skilled at reconciling the dimensions of all the ready-made elements of the earlier Parthenon to the overall requirements of his own building plan. In his restructuring of the Parthenon, he made the major lines of it conform to a proportional ratio of 9:4.[18]   The ratio of the length to the width of the stylobate, the stylobate width at the east and west ends to the height to the cornice over it, and the relationship of the spacing of the pillar centres to the pillar diameter at the base, are all seemingly in this numerical ratio. To the human eye these ratios are never perceptible, being distorted by perspective, the effects of scale and the distance of the viewer from the temple, yet they must have meant something to Iktinos.   Architects have always hankered after such mystiques, believing they promote a harmony within their creations, while they are really only devices of dimensional convenience.   On the earlier Parthenon, judging from the archaeological evidence, the relationship between the axial spacing and the pillar diameter had been, on the telling flank, the same as that between the pillar height and the axial spacing. The table, figure 77, shows similar corresponding ratios on the major Doric temples built in the first three quarters of the fifth century: note, on the Aigina temple, the close similarity of ratios C, D and G, and the 2:1 relationship of A and B; on the Temple of Zeus at Olympia, the 2:1 relationship of A and B, and E to F, and within D itself; the lack of them on the Hephaisteion apart from the simple ones of C and E; the near misses on the Temple of Apollo at Bassai of so many ratios, A (front), C (front), F, G, and H, all based on thirds and sixths, which correspond in some degree with those at Olympia A and B, which are also close to relationships of sixths.

The predilection for ratios of thirds and sixths may indicate a possible link in tradition of Iktinos with Olympia.   Perhaps, as Dinsmoor suggested,[19] Iktinos had served an apprenticeship with

---

[18] More precisely, $\sqrt{5}:1$, according to Demetrios Papageorgiou, which is certainly a concept more Greek than Roman, although the simple Roman ratio is more accurate when applied to the stylobate dimensions as measured by Penrose.
[19] 'A.A.G.' 1950 p.154.

Fig. 77 PROPORTIONS WITHIN TEMPLE DESIGNS. A comparative table

		Mentor of Kallikrates	Kallikrates	Mentor of Iktinos	Iktinos	Iktinos	Kallikrates as mentor
		Temple of Aphaia at Aegina	Old Parthenon	Temple of Zeus at Olympia	Parthenon	Temple of Apollo at Bassae	Temple of Hephaisteion (Theseum)
A	axial spacing / col diameter	front 2.65 / flank 2.59	front 2.44 / flank 2.35	2.32 / 2.37	2.25	2.34 / 2.38	2.54
B	col height / col diameter	5.32	5.54	4.64 / 4.72	5.48	5.13 / 5.31	5.61
C	height of entablature / col diameter	1.99 / 2.06	1.73	1.81 / 1.88	1.73	1.67 / 1.74	1.98 / 1.95
D	col height / axial spacing	2.01 / 2.05	2.27 / 2.35	2.00 / 1.99	2.43	2.19 / 2.23	2.21
E	height of order / axial spacing	2.76 / 2.86	2.98 / 3.09	2.78 / 2.79	3.19	2.91 / 2.96	2.99 / 2.98
F	height of order / col height	1.37 / 1.39	1.31	1.39 / 1.40	1.32	1.33	1.35
G	stylobate length / stylobate width	2.092	2.803	2.316	2.25	2.64	2.317
H	stylobate width / height of order	1.902	1.76	1.907	2.25	1.831	1.77

Values of simple ratios

$\dfrac{2}{1}=2$ $\dfrac{4}{3}=1.33$ $\dfrac{7}{4}=1.75$ $\dfrac{7}{5}=1.4$ $\dfrac{10}{6}=1.66$ $\dfrac{17}{7}=2.43$

$\dfrac{7}{3}=2.33$ $\dfrac{9}{4}=2.25$ $\dfrac{14}{5}=2.8$ $\dfrac{11}{6}=1.833$

$\dfrac{8}{3}=2.66$ $\dfrac{11}{4}=2.75$ $\dfrac{14}{6}=2.33$

Libon, the architect of the Zeus temple. and was, like him, from Elis. Perhaps his primary skills were in woodworking rather than in masonry. If Iktinos had built the demountable framework for Pheidias's statue of Zeus, that could explain his arrival in Athens when Pheidias was being commissioned for a similar work there. If Kallikrates had been the architect of the earlier Parthenon, his age would have been the reason for presenting Iktinos with the unexpected invitation to rebuild what was to become the most famous temple in history. The subsequent story of Iktinos seems to support this proposition. Instead of being asked to build the new gateway at the entrance to the Akropolis, he was sent away from the city in 438 BC to carry out another programme of enlargement, one he never completed, this time to the Hall of the Mysteries at Eleusis. He may have become tainted, in some Athenian eyes, as a foreigner and a friend of Pheidias, in the political shenanigans surrounding the trial of the famous sculptor. The Propylaia project was entrusted to Mnesikles, who must have worked with Iktinos on the Parthenon, for his work on the Propylaia is so closely related to the details of the temple.

Kallikrates and Pheidias had provided Iktinos with an opportunity given to few architects - to modify a building already in existence, one which possessed details of exquisite subtlety and boldness. While Iktinos was not capable of creating them, he could copy them; but when he tried to invent new forms, as he did in the interior at Bassai, if Pausanias's attribution is correct, the quirky version of the Ionic capitals and bases which he produced revealed that he was not so gifted. It was probably Pheidias who called for the increase on the rise of the curvature on the Parthenon stylobate, the greater angle of lean on the pillars and walls, and a welcoming of the idea of 'irregulae' on the architrave beams, bringing rubato into the rhythm of the exterior frieze.   As a sculptor Pheidias knew that inert material could be brought to life by the nuances of form given to it.   These were consciously endowed by the artist, but they operated at a subliminal level on the observer.   They were the fine tuning which made it possible for the Parthenon to sing throughout the centuries, while most other buildings simply slept the time away.

(5)   The role of Pheidias.

In Plutarch's day the tradition that Pheidias was the final authority in artistic matters was still firm enough for it to be written down by him in unequivocal terms.   If the weight of that authority could bring about the taking down of an almost completed temple in order to accommodate the figure of Athene he was commissioned to make, then that fact alone establishes the measure of Pheidias's reputation in Athens at the beginning of the 440's.   It would explain also the depth of enmity held towards him by those aristocratic conservatives in Athens whose families had contributed over many years to the cost of the building which he and Perikles appeared to destroy; for to Perikles would fall the task of persuading the Assembly to embark on this controversial aspect of his general plan, bold enough in itself, to rebuild the rest of the holy places in Attika desecrated by the Persians more than thirty years earlier.   Here were sown the seeds of Pheidias's downfall, his trials for embezzlement and impiety, his imprisonment and his death in custody.   That seems to be the account of what happened which was most favoured at the time of Plutarch's writing on the subject although, familiar with the rival accounts of history, he acknowledged that in all such matters *"the truth"* is unclear.

How had Pheidias earned such overwhelming prestige by 448 BC?   The order in which he carried out the known works attributed to him is not at all certain.   His career as a sculptor is punctuated by a series of enormous projects, each of them lasting several years, during which he must also have created numerous important but relatively smaller commissions.   A figure of Athene Areia at Plataia, of gilded wood with extremities carved in Pentelic marble, was reputed to be little smaller than the bronze Athene Promakhos which stood 17 metres tall, including its plinth, on the Athenian Akropolis.   The accounts for the latter stretch over nine years but have yet to be reliably dated.   The Athene Parthenos alone can be securely placed between 448 and 438 BC. but there is dispute over whether his most famous product, the seated Zeus at Olympia, was carried out before 448 or after Pheidias's trial in 438/7,   for an alternative version of the outcome of that alleges that he was disgraced and fled to Elis, where he worked on the Zeus.

Is it likely that Pheidias would have been entrusted with the Zeus at Olympia after suffering such a humiliation and possible loss of citizenship in Athens following the dedication of his statue to Athene in 438 BC?   The opinions of his enemies, the rivals of Perikles, would have carried even more weight in influential circles in Olympia than in Athens at the time.   Thoukudides, son of Melesias of Alopeke,[20] a kinsman by marriage of Kimon and therefore a member of one of those families whose gifts towards the cost of the earlier Parthenon would have appeared to be needlessly squandered by Pheidias, had himself been ostracised by the Athenians in 443.   He had led the criticism of Perikles's building plans, which he considered a gross misuse of the funds of the Delian league.[21]   Some believe he had been

---

[20] Not the historian of that name, who was the son of Olorus, although it was suggested by Cavaignac that Olorus had married the older Thoukudides's daughter.
[21] The political struggle between Perikles and Thoukudides has been seen as a personal rivalry, but defining it at that level is to leave out of account the events of the early 440's when Perikles persuaded the Assembly that, as part of his proposed

Cont'd

elected one of the generals in the one year when Perikles was not, but it may have been the case that Perikles, having been made responsible to the Assembly for the supervision of the finances of the building projects which he had promoted, declined to stand that year in order to concentrate on seeing off his opponent in a contest culminating in ostracism for one of them at a time when such rivalries at home were at their peak. Whatever the background, Thoukudides had powerful friends in the Peloponnese who would have seen to it that Pheidias was not trusted with large quantities of gold and ivory to work on a statue of Zeus, following any disgrace in Athens.   And yet Pheidias's name was inscribed under the feet of Zeus, describing the artist as an Athenian.   It seems more likely that it was the Zeus, fashioned between 456 and 448 BC, which established Pheidias as such a formidable talent in the Greek world, one whose subsequent outrageous recommendations in Athens would not be questioned by the majority of the people. Moreover, why would the priesthood of Zeus wait twenty years after completing the temple at Olympia before commissioning the figure of the god to inhabit it?   And, if that was the time sequence, why would Pheidias be unable to persuade them to enlarge their temple too, as he had successfully done at Athens? Strabo cannot have been alone in thinking the Zeus grossly out of scale with the interior of the temple.

---

spending programme of rebuilding the many temples and shrines throughout Attika which had been desecrated by the Persians in 479-80 and not yet restored, the Temple of Athene on the Akropolis, nearing completion, should be taken down and rebuilt in a widened form.   So soon after the death of Kimon this must have appeared to the members of the wealthier families of Athens as a serious affront.   They had largely paid for the temple, and no doubt were beginning to bask in the glamour and self-satisfaction of seeing this expression of their pride almost accomplished.   Perikles's action provided a fierce focus of the political antagonism; it would have been seen by his opponents as an act of cultural piracy, and was certainly one with dire consequences, initially for Thoukudides and later, on the latter's return to Athens in 433 BC, for his enemy Perikles.

A more credible ordering of Pheidias's work would place his Athene Areia at Plataia, a work relatively modest in the material employed, as the first of his large commissions, with the long running series of bronze heroes for Delphi close to it, if not preceding it in date.   The heroes depicted included Miltiades, whose son Kimon therefore probably commissioned at least one of them, and he is possibly the patron too for the huge bronze Athene Promakhos on the Athenian Akropolis, a work whose fame would be enough to ensure Pheidias's employment at Olympia, before he was invited back to Athens to make the Athene for the temple which then was approaching completion.

The evidence cited in support of Pheidias working at Olympia in the mid-430's is not strong.   A throwaway remark by Pausanias in his description of the Zeus, written around 150 AD, *"They say that the youth binding a fillet on his head resembles Pantarkes, an Elean boy who Pheidias loved.   Pantarkes won a victory in the boys wrestling contest during the 86th Olympiad"* (436 BC), could be no more than the fanciful tale of Pausanias's guide, oblivious of the significance to be put on it by later scholars with a sense of chronology more developed than his own.   Remains of casting moulds for drapery, assumed to have come from Pheidias's workshop were, according to Bundgaard,[22] among other material brought together by later levelling of the ground, so confounding any attempt to date this material reliably by proximity with other finds.   With a large team of modellers, carvers, and foundrymen such as Pheidias needed to have around him to carry out his multifarious commissions, he was likely to leave behind in Olympia, as well as his cup - one of the finds - a number of his workers to finish off other less prestigious projects.   The moulds were apparently for a female figure less grandiose in conception than the Zeus.   Even in Pausanias's day there were men at

---

[22] Bundgaard 'Parthenon and the Mycenean City on the Heights' 1976 p.192 n.343.

Olympia described as Pheidias's *"descendants"*, who were still employed in regular cleaning of the ivory and gold figure in the temple.

Pheidias's concept for his figure of Zeus had been a stroke of genius.   Faced with the daunting task of making the image of the great god in a temple which was already completed, where only parts of the figure could pass through the doorway, he exploited the claustrophobic interior at Olympia to increase the impression of the immensity of Zeus himself.   He constructed him with prefabricated sections, sat him on a throne and made the whole assembly such an overwhelming size that the head of the figure reached the roof, giving the impression that Zeus had always been there and that the temple must have been built around him; moreover, if he were to stand up, the temple would burst apart, for Zeus, Pheidias's Zeus, was greater than the temple.

At Athens the problem of fitting a large statue into the earlier Parthenon would have been the same as at Olympia, an interior dominated by two rows of superimposed pillars, because they defined a space more than twice as high as the clear width.   But Athene needed space around her; she had to be seen from every angle, her presence was not intended to terrify the viewer but to inspire awe and reverence.   Widening the interior dimension to one and a half times its former width shifted the pillars away from her figure and, returning the line of them behind it defined another space independent of the walls, within which she could command respect and wonder,[23] a generous space in extreme contrast to the way sculpture was used on the exterior of the temple.   It was the exact opposite of the arrangement at Olympia,

---

[23] The effect of this can once more be seen in the full size replica of the interior at Nashville, Tennessee.

Fig. 78 PROPORTIONS OF INTERIORS COMPARED

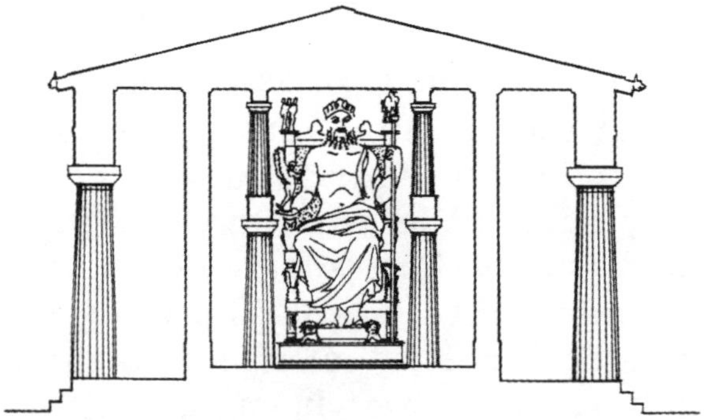

Pheidias's Zeus in the temple at Olympia 448 BC

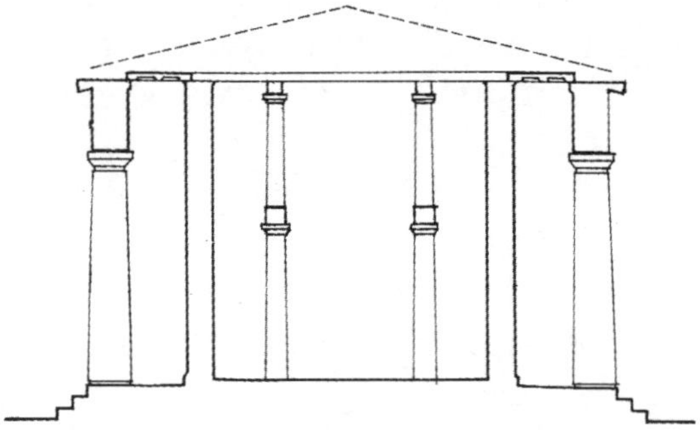

Design of the unfinished temple at Athens 448 BC

Pheidias's Athene in the Parthenon at Athens 438 BC

where he had crowded the interior for maximum effect, but also, one suspects, in protest against the use, on the exterior there, of sculpture as a subservient art to fill voids in the architecture, where even details of the hair on the figures was, it seems, felt to be inappropriate and therefore suppressed, to avoid conflict with the severe lines of the building.

Clearly, Pheidias had a new vision of the relationship between sculpture and architecture, which was the outcome of his experience at Olympia.   For him, sculpture was the master art, capable not only of enlivening the lines of the architecture, but also of expressing ideas which architecture alone could not. Beyond the purely plastic impact of the temple which we experience now, even in its sadly depleted form, there were, for contemporary Athenians, other levels of meaning embodied in the Parthenon by Pheidias, representational meanings, something akin to the meaning of the words of a poem which relate to, but most of all give point to, their sound and rhythm. Some of these meanings, conveying new perceptions of man and his relationship to the gods, of the polis in relation to the cosmos, were inspiring; others were profoundly subversive and these were to earn for Pheidias the serious charge of impiety.

The enlargement of the structure of the temple, from 6 x 16 pillars around the perimeter to 8 x 17, required more metopes there as well as more pillars.   Those used in the earlier Parthenon over the inner row of pillars at the east and west ends were the same height and the same width as those over the exterior peristyle, and it was probably a happy coincidence that all together they made up the exact number needed for the peristyle frieze of Iktinos's revised plan.   Some re-arrangement of these features would have been required, including bringing two extra metopes to each long flank.   A few years before the disastrous explosion which destroyed the Parthenon in 1687, brought about by a Venetian shell hitting the temple which was being used by the Turks as an arsenal, a French draughtsman, Jacques Carrey, had made the only record which exists of the arrangement of the south flank metopes. Carrey's drawings show, in the centre section of the south side, two alternative myths of how the Kentaurs came into being, (a sure sign that a committee of advisors was at work in the 460's). Metopes 19 and 20 in Carrey's numbering[24] appear to have nothing to do with the subject matter, and they must be the two transferred from elsewhere, a public act of disdain which signalled that those now making these decisions wished it to be known that such myths were devalued. Pheidias could have commissioned two more groups of Kentaur/Lapith struggles to maintain the integrity of the story but, for whatever reason, he did not. It is even possible that the story of Boreas, the north wind, would have been originally located on the north flank of the earlier Parthenon and was switched by Pheidias to the less prominent south side where fewer people would see it.

Figure 79 shows a reconstruction of the arrangement of the sculptures in the pediments, based on existing fragments and Carrey's drawings. There is no drawing recording the central section of the pediment at the east end. The figures are thought to have illustrated the phenomenal birth of Athene, the virgin goddess. Here, presumably, the scene was dominated by Zeus, but whether seated or standing is not certain. It would have included Athene sprung fully formed from the head of Zeus, released by the blow of an axe wielded by the lame Hephaistos. Several of the figures to either side have survived and they show the huge stylistic leap which was made, when compared with the

---

[24] T.Bowie and D.Thimme 'The Carrey Drawings of the Parthenon Sculptures' Bloomington-London 1971.

Fig. 79 ARRANGEMENT OF PEDIMENT SCULPTURES

East

West

Fig 80 SOUTH METOPES NUMBERS 13—24 DRAWN BY CARREY

South Metopes 13—16

13
Zeus forgiving Ixion

14
Ixion seducing Nephele

15
Kentauros siring two
Magnesian mares

16
Hermes scourging Ixion

South Metopes 17—20

17
Boreas attempting to seduce
Oreithyia

18
Boreas asking Erechtheus for
the hand of Oreithyia

19
Metopes transferred from inner frieze.

20

South Metopes 21–24

21
The shrine to Boreas with
Erechtheus and Oreithyia

22
Kentaur assaulting a Lapith
maiden

23

24
Kentaurs and Lapiths fighting

figures which occupied previous pediments on the Akropolis. They are rendered in a way so realistic as to accent their humanity over their divinity; figures K, L and M might be Aspasia and friends, who have laboured up the steeply ramped way to the site, perspiring with the effort and having arrived, glad to rest, their thin chitons wet and clinging to their shoulders, breasts, bellies and thighs.   These manage to be images of erotic and lasting beauty, the like of which had never been seen before, and to find them on the temple pediment must have caused astonishment at the time of their unveiling.

The composition is built on layers of irony.   Zeus, having devoured his first wife Metis, fearing she would bring forth a son greater than himself, took Hera to wife and fathered a gifted cripple Hephaistos, the ugliest of the gods by all accounts.   But he alone among the Olympian family could make things of beauty and utility.   He, the artist, is the one who had the courage to assault the terrible Zeus, intending to relieve his headache with an axe, only to deliver a splendid virgin goddess, Athene, even more gifted than himself, whom he would lust after in the days to come.   The other residents of Olympos shown to left and right of this devastating event seemed scarcely to notice it, being so absorbed in themselves and each other.   The expression is unequivocal.   Only Athene comes out of it well, for she embodied all the virtues which Perikles and his friends were trying to persuade the Athenians could be theirs.   In Athens she alone, who gave her name to the city, was to represent all that was pure, all that was virtuous, noble and generous.   She was the teacher in the arts of war, wise, prudent, always preferring the arts of peace, husbandry of land and family.   She was the valued patron of wit, music, dancing and all human creativity.

Was Pheidias seen, or did he see himself, as the contemporary embodiment of Hephaistos, bringing all these qualities into public prominence by a single blow of his axe to the head of the old religion?   In the eyes of the conservative opposition, was this his second and greatest act of impiety?

Is there a black hole in our understanding of the complexity of Athenian religion in the middle of the 5th century BC., caused by the disappearance of Herodotos's other historical work dealing with Assyria, to which he refers in Book 1.183?   The content of this, even if not yet committed to a text, must have been a topic of conversation in Perikles's circle of friends while Herodotos resided in Athens, and the intelligentsia of the time would have known about the two phases of the return of the Israelites from Babylon sanctioned by Cyrus and Artaxerxes - Nehemiah certainly and Ezra possibly were contemporaries of Perikles – and they would have known too, no doubt, something of the singular Jewish God Yahweh.   The implications of the testimony of Anaxagoras that in the beginning there was Nous, and the unfolding belief in the possibility that men could be capable of comprehending the nature of the universe by using their own minds, seem to have been left out of the accounts of Athenian religion around the middle of the 5th century.   The Athenians were the least insular of people, and they traded with the known world in more than goods.   Early in the century Themistokles had ignored the advice of the oracle and trusted his own insight into how to defeat the Persian fleet at Salamis.   He was guided by his mentor Mnesophilos who perhaps reminded him of how, in Homer's 'Iliad', Nestor had recounted the method by which Lykourgos had lured King Areithous, the mace-man, into a narrowly confined cleft in a rock where his terrifying weapon was useless, a strategy which, when repeated, defeated the Persian allied fleet at Salamis.

It is noteworthy that since the colossal temple to Zeus was started below the Akropolis by the sons of Peisistratos, and abandoned when Hippias fled into exile, no attempt was made to resume the building of that temple to the father of the gods, by either Kimon or Perikles. The size of the temple, requiring pillars of 2.4m diameter, may have been decided at the wishes of the tyrants, and it may be that no-one was technically competent enough to continue and complete it for another three hundred years. It seems more likely that, in the eyes of Perikles and his friends, Zeus had become identified with all that the demos feared and detested. In Athens at this time, public honour and homage were concentrated on Athene to a remarkable degree.

Although there were problems in reducing the metope voids allowed in the new design for the Parthenon to accommodate the already existing metopes, Pheidias made a virtue of them, as he had done in the interior at Olympia. The fighting figures appear to be bursting out of the confining architecture in which they were now set, instead of being, as they would have been before, a series of separately framed pictures. This artistic theme - a favourite of Pheidias's at the time, as we have seen - of compression and crowding, he brought to perfection in the Parthenon naos wall frieze. Here layer upon layer, as many as seven in places within a shallow relief, of horses and men overlapped one another, anticipating polyphony, to make a dynamic drive, barely interrupted in its flow of over 160 metres from west to east. It was an idea which broke the confines of his own art as surely as his horses' heads overhung the pedimental cornices within which they could not be contained. In his day the frieze must have appeared like a song or an epic poem in stone, so extended was the experience of it, that it began to occupy the dimension of time as well as space.

Fig. 81 PART OF THE WEST FRIEZE AS DRAWN BY CARREY AND AS ASSEMBLED FROM CASTS

West Frieze VIII-X

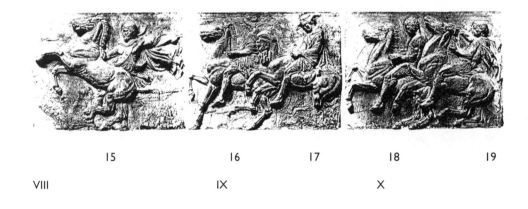

<table>
</table>

		15		16		17		18		19

VIII   IX   X

Ian Jenkins[25] has illustrated the subject matter and described the many possible complex and subtle interpretations of it succinctly.   The portrayal of the most popular Athenian religious festival in the frieze was at once a bold and eccentric concept, yet the idea had won the approval not only of Perikles, but also the priesthood and, no doubt, the visiting committee of the Boule, for they would represent the whole Assembly in making such decisions.   To set in stone this image of the ordinary Athenian, acting in unison with his friends and kinsmen in an act of worship was unusual enough, but to place it where it so plainly supported the roof of this great temple, protecting Athene herself, the protector of the city, from all the god-sent elements, must have held a powerful appeal for the democratic instincts of all called upon to fulfil a role in the administration of Athens.   The frieze was expressing in stone that the ordinary people, no longer fearful, but acting with the gods in friendship, had a part to play, a responsibility for their own actions in supporting and maintaining the security of their polis within the cosmic order. And that part was essentially peaceful, attending to the fruitful earth, and celebrating its gifts in contest, song and sacrifice.

This new friendship of men and gods was represented at the east end of the frieze, where the gods were seated in receptive mood in Athens, though by their demeanour they might be at home on Olympos, waiting to be entertained by the citizens taking part in the procession. The ambiguity of the occasion is intriguing. Athenian marshals appear to be in charge of the proceedings although the gods are present. Roles are reversed and yet both men and gods appear relaxed. Is this a new relationship of amity that can be born of peace? Are gods made angry only by mortal disagreement?   If men make peace, can all life be a festival? All this was said or implied in stone, without triumphalism, over the

---

[25] Ian Jenkins 'The Parthenon Frieze' 1994.

Fig. 82 PART OF THE EAST FRIEZE AS DRAWN BY CARREY AND AS ASSEMBLED FROM CASTS

East Frieze Eight of the eleven figures of VI

	38		39		40		41	42		43	44	45

VI Poseidon   Apollo   Artemis   Aphrodite   Eros   Magistrates

very door to Athene's temple.   There has never been a more eloquent expression in artistic form of the noble sentiments which provided the dynamic to the idea of democracy.   Tucked away in its appropriate place on the temple, avoiding hubris, it still revealed the motives of an entire generation of men, brilliant leaders of opinion, of civic sensibility and artistic excellence, who had an insight into how men might govern themselves, act creatively, not merely for private gain but honourably, as part of a vigorous community of which they were not only content but proud to be a part.   Aristeides, Ephialtes, Perikles, Anaxagoras, Protagoras, Aiskhulos. Sophokles, Euripides, Pheidias, Agorakritos, Damon, Kallikrates, Herodotos and the later historian Thucydides were all, as individuals and collectively, manifestations of how glorious life can be within its own acknowledged tragedy.   Some of these men were poets who, like others before them, raised the regular festival recitations which remembered past heroes, transforming them into drama, revising Greek theology in the process, portraying passion and compassion in language which resonated with the deepest feelings known to all the citizens, themselves incapable of voicing them.   Others worked stone to make the figures and the buildings which were renowned from the moment they were finished and keep their magnetism still, possessing a value which surmounts every cultural barrier since erected by lesser men.   In some ways the most remarkable of all, because so many of them were relatively self-effacing, are those we know only as politicians or contributors to debate, who provided the wise and enlightened patronage which made these lasting works possible, and from whom there is still so much to learn about their own art of government, in particular their attempts to devise a faction-free assembly open to every citizen, where discussion and argument were employed to arrive at appropriate decisions, rather than to win and wield power over their fellow men.   It is undeniable that the part these gifted men played was a distinguished one, but the distinction flowed not merely from their association with the institutions, the Assembly or the guilds and festivals to which they contributed, but from the quality of the personal gifts they brought to their roles, and the spirit of accountable freedom within which they could practice them.

Within thirty years the bright vision had faded, Democracy was deified and worshipped; it is worshipped still, 2400 years later; it is still misunderstood by people equating representative government with democracy, but it is believed in firmly enough for believers to wage war in order to impose this false version of it on sometimes reluctant people. Only the ideas and the artifacts sustain the true memory of it.   It would still profit us to try harder to understand them.

Fig. 83 ROUTES OF THE PERSIAN INVADERS IN 490 AND 480 BC

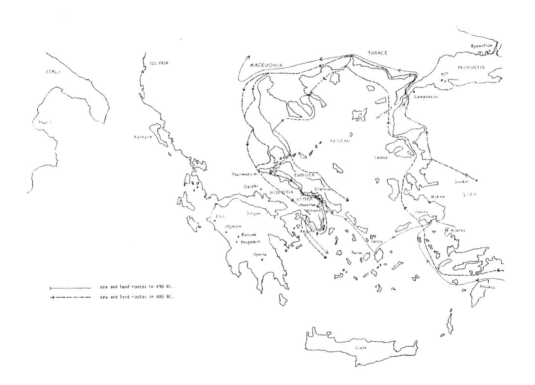